PET Practice Tests 2

Teacher's Book

*Diana L. Fried-Booth and
Louise Hashemi*

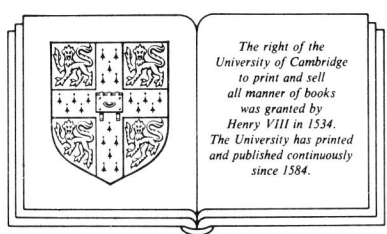

Cambridge University Press
Cambridge
New York   Port Chester
Melbourne   Sydney

Published by the Press Syndicate of the University of Cambridge
The Pitt Building, Trumpington Street, Cambridge CB2 1RP
40 West 20th Street, New York, NY 1011-4211, USA
10 Stamford Road, Oakleigh, Melbourne 3166, Australia

© Cambridge University Press 1991

First published 1991

**Printed in Great Britain by
Scotprint Ltd., Musselburgh**

ISBN 0 521 356806 paperback Student's Book
ISBN 0 521 356814 paperback Teacher's Book
ISBN 0 521 355907 Set of 2 cassettes

Copyright
The law allows a reader to make a single copy of part of a book for purposes of private study. It does not allow the copying of entire books or the making of multiple copies of extracts. Written permission for any such copying must always be obtained from the publisher in advance.

Contents

Thanks   *iv*

Introduction   *1*

The Preliminary English Test   *2*

What is the PET?   *2*

The syllabus   *2*

The structure of the PET   *3*

Question formats and aims   *3*

Mark scheme   *5*

Using *PET Practice Tests*   *7*

The Oral   *15*

Frameworks for conducting the Oral   *20*

Visual material for the Oral: *colour section at centre of book*

Answer keys   *38*

Unit 1   Shopping and services   *38*

Unit 2   Health and medicine   *47*

Unit 3   Travel and tourism   *55*

Unit 4   Family, education and society   *62*

Unit 5   PET practice test paper   *70*

Thanks

We should like to thank all the students and staff at the various schools where the material for *PET Practice Tests 2* was piloted who took the time and trouble to record their comments and reactions. Particular thanks also to the students and staff at The Chichester School of English who contributed towards producing 'sample' answers for the final version of the Teacher's Book. We are also indebted to Jeanne McCarten and Annie Cornford for their encouragement and support during the writing and revision of this material.

Acknowledgements
The author and publishers wish to acknowledge the following:
Colour oral section: photographs by Howard Fried-Booth (1B, 1C, 2A), Jeremy Pembrey (2B, 2C, 3B, 3C, 4C, 4D); artwork by Mike Hingley (3A) and David Mostyn (1A, 5B).

Introduction

This book of PET Practice Tests is designed to provide practice for potential PET candidates. It has been organised thematically so that test practice can be integrated into the teacher's ordinary lesson plans. This has the advantage of greater flexibility in planning for the teacher, as the work done will be of value to students who are not intending to take the PET as well as to those who are. Each of the first four units is based on a theme likely to be of relevance to learners at this level. The fifth unit replicates the PET itself in that it is non-thematic and can therefore be used as a mock test just before the PET is taken.

The Preliminary English Test

WHAT IS THE PET?

The Preliminary English Test – PET – was introduced by the University of Cambridge Local Examinations Syndicate (UCLES) in 1980 and was substantially revised in 1987.

The PET is a test in three parts intended for students who have studied English for approximately 300–350 hours and have reached a basic level of communicative competence in reading, writing, listening and speaking. Each of these skills is of equal importance, as is indicated by the way the test is marked (see below p. 3). The PET is considered by UCLES to be about two-thirds of the way towards the First Certificate in English.

THE SYLLABUS

The syllabus for the PET is closely related in content and level to the Council of Europe's Threshold Level*. A success in the PET should indicate that the student has the language skills to cope socially at a 'survival' level in an English-speaking country. This implies the ability to:

> identify him/herself
> identify other people
> make and reply to requests, offers, suggestions
> give directions
> say where things are
> talk about time
> give information about things
> discuss likes and dislikes
> discuss his/her needs
> discuss what people are doing

The student should also know language related to:

> personal identification (name, address, date of birth etc.)
> accommodation (where he/she lives, type of house/flat etc.)
> home life (family, occupation, daily routine etc.)

---

* *The Threshold Level for Modern Language Learning in Schools*, J. A. van Ek (Longman, 1976).

education and future career (school examinations, career intentions etc.)
free time, entertainment (hobbies, interests, radio, cinema, TV etc.)
travel (public and private transport, holidays, fares etc.)
health and welfare (parts of the body, illness, accidents, medical and insurance services etc.)
relations with other people (friendship, invitation, letter-writing etc.)
shopping (facilities, goods, prices, weights etc.)
food and drink (types of food and drink, restaurants etc.)
services (post, telephone, bank, police, repairs etc.)
places (using a map, asking and giving directions etc.)
weather (climate, weather conditions etc.)
foreign language (assessing ability, asking for clarification, correction etc.)

THE STRUCTURE OF THE PET

Reading and Writing Paper $1\frac{1}{2}$ hours
Listening Paper $\frac{1}{2}$ hour (approx.)
Speaking   8–10 minutes (depending on individual/pair)

The test is divided into four areas of assessment; reading, writing, listening and speaking, each of which carries 25% of the total marks. The marks for Questions 1–5 will not necessarily add up to 25. The raw mark, however, is scaled so that it represents 25% of the total mark. For example if the total mark is 32 the following scaling would apply:

Raw Mark: 1 2 3 4 5 6 7 8 9 10 11 12 13 14 15 16 17 18 19 20
Scaled Mark: 1 2 2 3 4 5 5 6 7   8   9   9 10 11 12 13 13 14 15 16

Raw Mark: 21 22 23 24 25 26 27 28 29 30 31 32
Scaled Mark: 16 17 18 19 20 20 21 22 23 23 24 25

The same process is applicable (if necessary) to the Writing Skills, Questions 6–8, and to the Listening Skills, Questions 9–12.

Questions 1–8 form one complete paper. Questions 9–12 and the Oral form two further separate parts. The texts for the Listening are only available on cassette. The Oral may be taken before or after the other parts of the test.

In each part of the test the questions are graded both in terms of difficulty and level of skill required.

QUESTION FORMATS AND AIMS

READING

Question 1
This consists of five multiple choice questions testing comprehension of public notices or signs.

The Preliminary English Test

Question 2
A short reading passage with ten gaps which are designed to test vocabulary in context, structural points, and appreciation of the meaning of the passage beyond sentence level. The answer format is multiple choice.

Question 3
This tests the student's ability to retrieve detailed information of a factual nature from a variety of texts. The material will be straightforward, possibly incorporating visuals, with very little redundancy. There will be between five and ten questions of the True/False, box-ticking, matching, grid-filling type.

Question 4
This is likely to use texts based on advertisements, public notices, brochures or leaflets. It aims to test the ability to scan for specific information of a factual nature. The texts will be fuller and contain much more redundant material than those for Question 3, although the format and number of questions may be similar.

Question 5
This uses a text chosen to reflect a combination of fact and opinion in order to test gist comprehension. There will normally be five questions: the first two are multiple choice and designed to test understanding of the source of the passage and the writer's intention; the next two are open-ended, requiring answers of up to sentence length; the final question usually presents some additional information in words or visual images and aims to test ability to compare information in the text with related material presented in a different form.

WRITING

Question 6
The five sub-questions all fall within one context such as hotels, clothing or shopping. The student has to transform the structure of one sentence into another sentence without losing the meaning of the original.

Question 7
This involves directed writing based on a stimulus which gives the student a clear framework for the answer. There may be one exercise, or two which are related in content, for example, filling in a booking form and then a message to give details of the booking to a friend. Tasks such as making notes, filling in forms or writing messages are set and up to 75 words may be required altogether.

Question 8
This involves 'free' writing with a stimulus as a clear starting point, but allowing the student to use some imagination. The tasks are based on situations likely to be relevant to the student, for example, a simple narrative of recent experiences, description of future plans, statement of opinion or request for information. About 100 words are required.

Mark scheme

LISTENING

Each question will be heard twice.

Half a minute is allowed between Questions 9 and 10, and a minute between 10 and 11, and 11 and 12, for students to check their answers.

Question 9
There are seven multiple choice items, each consisting of either a short dialogue (of up to four lines), or a single utterance. The question format is entirely visual, using photographs, diagrams, sketch maps, pictograms etc.

Question 10
This contains largely factual information of a practical nature such as information about travel conditions or public announcements. Very little reading or writing is required. There will be about five or six questions in a box-ticking or multiple choice format.

Question 11
Here the material will usually be narrative or discursive in style containing information of general interest to the student. Likely sources are radio current affairs programmes, reports or talks. Approximately six questions are set, some of which will require short written answers: a word, a phrase or a number.

Question 12
This question, like Question 5, requires the student to demonstrate comprehension of gist and appreciation of opinions and attitudes. It takes the form of a short conversation with about five questions of the Yes/No or True/False type.

MARK SCHEME

Where the questions are multiple choice, marking is straightforward (see Answer keys). Where students are required to write in a word or a name, minor errors should not be penalised unless they prevent the marker from understanding the student's intention. For Questions 5–8 where questions are open-ended, guidance is given below and in the Answer keys where there are sample student answers with suggested marks.

Question 5
Sub-questions 1, 2 and 5 carry 1 mark each; sub-questions 3 and 4 normally carry two marks each.

In numbers 3 and 4 where students have to write short answers – usually only one or two sentences – allow two marks if the main idea is correct and is expressed in reasonably accurate language.

Question 6

In this question the transformation itself carries the marks. If other elements of the sentence have been wrongly copied, do not penalise the students.

Question 7

The mark for this question may vary slightly from one test to another. Half-marks (up to a total of 3–4 marks) may be awarded for appropriate completion of a task and 2–3 marks (up to a total of 5–6 marks) for the content and language used in completing the more open-ended tasks. The Answer keys provide the detailed breakdown for each Unit.

(NB Half-marks are rounded up before scaling.)

In awarding a mark for language skills, credit should be given for attempts to use structures that are appropriate, for example a letter which is required to make suggestions includes structures such as 'You should/ought to . . .' etc. In some cases single word answers or lists will be appropriate but in a section requiring more detail, full sentences may be expected, even though the structures may be limited and simple.

Question 8

This question carries 10 marks overall, 5 marks for completing the task and 5 marks for language. Students may be required to write both formal and informal letters and can expect to lose marks if a letter does not convey the correct tone and style. Letters should also begin and end appropriately. The same considerations apply to other tasks such as giving a simple report of an event, but initial guidance is always given in the form of an opening suggestion/prompt.

In awarding a mark for language skills, credit should be given to students who use a range of tenses and structures as well as demonstrating a command of vocabulary (appropriate to the level) in order to produce a piece of coherent natural-sounding prose.

Using *PET Practice Tests*

PET Practice Tests has been organised to allow teachers maximum flexibility having regard for the needs of their students, available teaching time and preferred teaching style.

STIMULUS AND PRACTICE

The questions in the book can be used as a source of stimulus and practice material for use in class and as homework. (For detailed suggestions on how to exploit each question type see pp. 8–14 below.)

INTEGRATED SKILLS

The theme of each of Units 1–4 can be used as the basis for project or other integrated skills work, incorporating different parts of the test as appropriate during the course of a week or fortnight. For example, different parts of each unit can be exploited to introduce or revise lexical items, to provide stimulus for written work or role play. This approach will be particularly beneficial where the class consists of a mixture of 'exam' and 'non-exam' students, who may need to be motivated in different ways to use the same materials.

INDIVIDUAL SKILLS AND REMEDIAL WORK

The different parts of the tests can be used in different skills lessons, or for individual study and remedial purposes. The best way to do this is to direct students through a series of similar exercises, for example in listening for detail, or for gist, or in guided compositions.

EXAMINATION PRACTICE

The book can be used as straightforward 'exam practice' material under test conditions. All the material is designed to be at the level of the PET, and can therefore be used in any order. Students can work through a series of tests at intervals during their course and gauge their progress as they become increasingly competent.

MOCK EXAMINATIONS

Unit 5 is purposely 'non-thematic' in order to provide a realistically mixed test which can be used as a mock exam if appropriate.

USING THE QUESTIONS

QUESTION 1

AIM

In this question the students are required to show that they understand public signs and notices. This is a survival skill, not only for the English-speaking areas of the world, but for many multi-lingual contexts, such as airports.

SUGGESTIONS FOR PREPARING YOUR STUDENTS

● Practice in this area can often be incorporated in work on imperative and passive structures.

● Notices often employ a 'telegram' language, omitting unimportant words. Some students will benefit from being shown examples of how this works, e.g. (Some) MEN (are) WORKING OVERHEAD.

● Where students are studying in an English-speaking country, encourage them to note examples of signs and notices that they see and set aside a short time each week to discuss them.

QUESTION 2

AIM

This type of exercise (a modified Cloze test) seeks to test the students' ability to deduce meanings from context in their general reading. The exercise is useful in training students to read words in groups and to take account of context when trying to understand the significance of a phrase.

Using the questions

SUGGESTIONS FOR PREPARING YOUR STUDENTS

● Although deducing meaning from context is an invaluable skill, the test format is one which many students find very daunting. In PET the multiple choice element gives students a certain amount of support. Following some of the steps outlined below may be useful if the students are having difficulties.

1 Before they tackle a whole passage, show the students some examples of sentences divided in half and jumbled. Ask them to match the beginnings and endings. Discuss with them how they achieved this. What were the 'clues'? Were they structural features such as tense, or lexical features to do with the subject content of the sentence?

2 Then look at short passages (two or three sentences in length) with one word missing. There's no need for multiple choice alternatives, as long as the text is simple. A good source will be material written by the students themselves, as this ensures that the language is really easy for them. At this stage you are trying merely to show them that it is easy to fill the gaps.

3 When they are confident, introduce more difficult examples. In discussing the answers, remind them frequently that the clues may be in the words preceding or following the gap or in the meaning of a previous or subsequent sentence.

QUESTION 3

AIM

In this question the students are being tested on their ability to understand a text in detail. They should not have to guess many words and should have a good idea of how the text works as a whole. This sort of reading comprehension exercise is well covered by many textbooks.

SUGGESTIONS FOR PREPARING YOUR STUDENTS

● Encourage the students to read the whole text carefully before looking at the questions, as the answers often require a synthesis of information from different parts of the text.

● Some students may find it helpful to make use of a pencil or highlighter to mark the key elements of each question and corresponding material in the text.

● To help students concentrate on detail in texts, it may be useful to try an exercise such as the following, which apart from being an enjoyable way to do reading comprehension, gives valuable practice in question formation.

1 Divide the class into halves or groups and give each group a different short passage. Ask them to write five questions on it.

2 The passages and questions are then exchanged and the groups have to find the answers.

3 The groups then hand back the questions with their answers and they 'mark' each other's work. (Points can also be deducted for linguistic errors in the questions.)

QUESTION 4

AIM

The skim reading skills that students must use for this question are different from the skills needed for Question 3. Here they must learn to disregard irrelevant material rather than analysing every detail. This may trouble some students who are not aware that they already employ a range of different reading skills in their first language.

SUGGESTIONS FOR PREPARING YOUR STUDENTS

● Advise the students to read the questions before looking at the text. This will allow them to skim the text looking for key words and phrases and avoid their having to work their way laboriously through all the redundant material.

● Ensure that students realise that they are not expected to understand every word of the text. Some conscientious students find this very hard to accept. In monolingual classes, it might be helpful to do a similar exercise in the mother tongue to demonstrate the point. Naturally, you may wish to study the test material in detail, but this should be a separate exercise and not done as practice for the test.

● If you have access to English-language newspapers, publicity material and so on, extra practice with materials on subjects of special interest to the students can be helpful.

QUESTION 5

AIM

The skills required for this question are the ability to grasp overall meaning combined with an awareness of style and register at the most simple level. As well as being important linguistic skills in a general sense, these skills will be very useful to students who take more advanced examinations later on.

SUGGESTIONS FOR PREPARING YOUR STUDENTS

● As far as identifying the source and intention of a text is concerned, clue hunting, through style as well as content, can be enjoyable and helpful. One way of starting this work with students is to provide sentences from a range of sources such as personal letters, advertisements, public information

Using the questions

leaflets, study notes and diaries. Invite the class to guess where you found them. This can be a team game, with points scored both for good guesses and correct identification of 'clues'.

● Even at this level, a few hints on register will be useful. For example, students should know that in English the pronoun 'you' is often used in an impersonal way, and may not indicate that the writer is addressing a specific reader, as it might in many languages. Another source of confusion to some students is short forms of verbs. The use of these in writing conveys an informality that the students may not be sensitive to, unless it is pointed out.

● Where students are asked a question or required to finish a sentence, their answers should be brief. The answers need never be more than two sentences long, and often much less will be adequate. Blind copying of a chunk of the text is not desirable. In fact, the questions are designed to encourage students to demonstrate their ability to communicate simple facts and ideas clearly, using their own words. Students who confuse quantity with quality will need a lot of practice in learning to do this exercise successfully.

QUESTION 6

AIM

This question is entirely a matter of structural accuracy. With care, most students should be able to make all the transformations correctly. The fact that the sentences are linked in sense should help students to understand each one.

SUGGESTIONS FOR PREPARING YOUR STUDENTS

● Some students find it helpful to practise identifying the task before attempting each transformation, for example whether it is a 'passive to active' or 'reported speech' question. It may be a good idea to incorporate exercises of this sort when practising new structures in class.

● If students find the concept of transformations problematic, the following exercise may help.

Choose some sentences which the students know well (e.g. from their own work). Write transformed versions and give these to the students, with the first word or two of the original sentence. The students, with help if necessary, will eventually produce their own original sentences. This exercise can later be developed into a game in which groups produce exercises for each other.

QUESTION 7

AIM

This question tests the students' ability to convey straightforward information in writing, often including filling in a form. There is very little invention required on the part of the students.

SUGGESTIONS FOR PREPARING YOUR STUDENTS

● Practice in writing should always begin at a simple level and this sort of exercise is very useful for this. Working in pairs may help students. Where it is possible for speakers of different first languages to be paired together, this may help as they will be better at spotting each other's linguistic weaknesses and may have a wider range of lexis between them.

● It is helpful if the teacher can collect plenty of examples of forms to fill in, so that students are used to giving information about themselves in English. This can also be tied in with initial practice for the Oral, Section I (see p. 16), where they may be asked similar questions.

● To provide students with authentic models for notes and messages, the teacher may try to keep all administrative notes etc. in English, where this is practicable, at any rate in the context of the classroom.

QUESTION 8

AIM

This question requires the students to produce connected prose, with the support of clearly defined aims and context.

SUGGESTIONS FOR PREPARING YOUR STUDENTS

● This, for most students, will prove more challenging than the previous exercise and may need more gradual preparation. Students should be encouraged to produce short, clear pieces with a minimum of errors. If they are making large numbers of mistakes, they are trying to do too much too soon. Take them back to working at sentence level for a while to regain confidence.

● If students complain that they can't think what to write, have class or group 'brain-storming' sessions, put the results on the board and show the students how to choose and order ideas before beginning to write.

● Some students have a lot of difficulty in controlling their language at the same time as using their imagination. It is never too early to start learning the discipline of:

i) Define your task
ii) Note down your ideas

Using the questions

iii) Put them in order
iv) Write
v) Check

This habit will be invaluable for more advanced language work.

QUESTION 9

AIM

Here the students are required to show that they understand a variety of spoken items such as announcements or brief exchanges. Students who have had plenty of practice in using and hearing English for everyday purposes will find this easier than those who have only been exposed to 'classroom' English, as they will have less difficulty 'tuning in' quickly.

SUGGESTIONS FOR PREPARING YOUR STUDENTS

● Before using the tape recording a lot of useful oral work can be done, which will provide a helpful preparation for the listening. Many of the sets of pictures can be examined for differences, and used to practise descriptions and comparisons.

● Working in pairs can be useful, requiring the students to argue through their choice of answer. If the students can use a language laboratory, each pair can have control of the recording and can progress at their own speed, rewinding and checking as necessary. This can be a great help in boosting confidence in the early stages.

● In monolingual classes, it will help if English is the only medium of communication, so that students become habituated to hearing English without a preamble in the mother tongue.

QUESTION 10

AIM

This question requires the students to pick out specific points of information from what they hear. This is the skill necessary for listening to information sources, where the listeners must be able to sift out irrelevancies and concentrate on their own particular needs or interests.

SUGGESTIONS FOR PREPARING YOUR STUDENTS

● If students find these longer pieces very daunting, it may help to compose one or two listening exercises similar to those in this book, but containing plenty of familiar references, for instance to events and locations known to the students, which can act as markers. From there it should be easier for the students to progress to similar exercises without familiar references, in the practice tests.

- There should be time for the students to cast their eyes over the questions before they hear the text. They should get into the habit of doing this as it will help them to listen for specific items of information.

- It may be worth warning students that ticking all the boxes will not result in getting at least half-marks – students who try this are penalised!

QUESTION 11

AIM

This question normally uses a more discursive style of text than Question 10, and will contain more redundant material. In addition, the students may well have to write one or two words for some of the answers. This is a study skill, which can form the basis of note-taking from lectures at a later stage.

SUGGESTIONS FOR PREPARING YOUR STUDENTS

- Exposure to a good variety of listening materials, for example on radio, is the best general preparation for this question.

- The texts may seem more difficult than those for Question 10, but the question will usually contain helpful clues, both in words and format, and students should be encouraged to make full use of this.

- Although inaccuracies are not to be encouraged, students can be reassured that, provided their answers are intelligible, minor errors will not count against them in listening comprehension questions, as it is their understanding which is being tested, not their writing skills.

QUESTION 12

AIM

In this question the student is required to infer facts and attitudes from what is said. Correct answers will demonstrate understanding of the text as a whole, rather than the ability to pick out specific points. This is a first step to more sophisticated techniques such as summarising and reporting.

SUGGESTIONS FOR PREPARING YOUR STUDENTS

- The most effective and enjoyable practice for this question will be working in groups or pairs, arguing through the True/False statements.

- Oral practice can be closely tied to these questions. Production and recognition of different intonation patterns will be particularly helpful and the conversations themselves can be used for models in oral work.

The Oral

In the PET, importance is attached to the balance of linguistic skills, and oral work should therefore not be neglected.

It is important to distinguish clearly between **examination practice**, in which students learn what to expect and how to perform at their best under interview conditions, and **preparation**, in which students acquire and practise oral skills, through a variety of classroom materials and activities. These skills will be needed for the purposes of general communication as well as for the examination.

The following notes have been prepared with reference to the instructions to PET Oral Examiners issued by UCLES in 1988. Teachers are advised to study them in conjunction with the Frameworks for conducting the Oral (see p. 20ff) in order that they may be able to familiarise their students with the structure and procedure of the test. Ideally, each candidate should be given at least one mock oral interview under examination conditions. A detailed description for the conduct of the Oral is given below in order to help the teacher play the part of the examiner as accurately as possible. Other than this, plenty of general oral work, covering the language areas described in the syllabus (see p. 2), and making use of the oral material provided in PET Practice Tests, will be of most value to the candidates.

STRUCTURE OF THE PET ORAL

The Oral consists of four Sections and lasts approximately ten minutes. The four Sections are not linked thematically, except that Section 4 is based on the visual material provided for Section 3*. The examiner will not announce the beginning or end of each Section but will probably say 'Thank you' at the end, and then go on to say what is to be done next.

Candidates take the Oral individually or in pairs. Sometimes an extra assessor sits in on the Oral, especially if there are candidates being examined in pairs.

---

* In Units 1–4 of *PET Practice Tests*, however, the themes are carried through (see Using *PET Practice Tests*, p. 7).

SECTION 1: GENERAL CONVERSATION

This part of the Oral will be much the same for all candidates. Although it is known as the 'warming-up' phase, it is fully assessed. The candidate must be able to give personal information, including spelling out one or two words. Top marks go to candidates who show the ability to initiate parts of the conversation, rather than merely respond accurately to questions.

SECTION 2: SIMULATED SITUATION

The candidate will be asked to perform a simple role simulation with the examiner or fellow student. The examiner describes the situation and, usually, gives the candidate a visual prompt, which may be a line drawing or a short piece of written material, for example a timetable or menu. The candidate(s) have a few moments preparation time before they have to speak. It is quite in order for candidates to check that they have correctly understood the instructions before they begin, by, for example, repeating what they have been asked to do.

SECTION 3: RESPONDING TO A VISUAL STIMULUS

The candidate is asked to describe and respond to a picture, normally a colour photograph. Lack of specialised vocabulary is not penalised, but good candidates will be expected to draw straightforward conclusions about the picture in addition to giving a factual description. There is no penalty for idiosyncratic interpretations of pictures, but candidates will have to justify them with simple explanations. For example 'I don't think this is England because the sun is shining', will be fine, even if the picture shows Trafalgar Square!

SECTION 4: GENERAL CONVERSATION BASED ON THE PHOTOGRAPH

Here the candidate is led to give information and opinions in conversation, without time being allowed for preparation. The examiner may well offer personal information or opinions for the candidate to respond to. The picture from Section 3 is used as a springboard for the discussion.

CONDUCT OF THE ORAL

The examiner will sit at a table, probably arranged at an angle to where the candidate(s) will sit. He or she will have the marksheets, and will write on them during the exam. The candidate(s) is/are not allowed to see these at any time.

The examiner will speak at a normal, but fairly slow, pace. If the candidate is nervous, or does not understand instructions, the examiner will repeat these extra slowly. The examiner may do more talking than in higher level oral examinations, in order to give plenty of support to the candidates, especially in Sections 1 and 4.

Candidates can expect the examiner to be patient and friendly but the examiner will not give the candidate any information about how well he or she has done. The examiner will not use expressions such as 'Good' or 'Fine', which candidates might interpret as a comment, nor will any errors be corrected or commented upon.

USE OF FRAMEWORK

Each Oral Test has a Framework of questions and remarks. At some points the examiner may simply pause after he or she has made a remark, to give the candidate an opportunity to initiate a part of the conversation. This is in order to try to avoid the traditional atmosphere of interrogation in oral examinations. The pause will not be allowed to go on too long if the candidate says nothing. The examiner will stick to the Framework as much as possible, but will be flexible in response to the candidate. When the candidate says something not provided for in the Framework, the examiner will allow the conversation to develop naturally. When this happens because the candidate has misunderstood, no indication will be given, but the examiner may try the question again at a later stage. If the candidate responds to the picture in Section 3 in such a way that the Framework for Section 4 is irrelevant, the examiner will try to lead the conversation so that it fits the language tasks for that part even though it does not match the subject matter.

TIMING

Section 1   Not more than 2 minutes
Section 2   Approximately 2 minutes
Sections 3 & 4   Approximately 4 minutes together

When a candidate completes the tasks for one Section in a shorter time, the examiner will go on to the next Section, allowing more time for that conversation.

Timing is the responsibility of the examiner. Candidates need not worry about it.

PAIR OPTION

Candidates may take the Oral in pairs. Some students find this very reassuring, especially if they are used to working together in class. It is important that they should be carefully matched. During the test, the examiner will give some help in Sections 1 and 4, but the candidates will be

The Oral

expected to talk mainly to each other in Sections 2 and 3. Material in Units 1–4 offers scope for practice of pairwork in orals.

ASSESSING ORAL PERFORMANCE

The candidate's performance is assessed both on the basis of achievement of task set and linguistic skills. Success in the task involves communication of the required message in an appropriate manner. The linguistic elements are structural accuracy, vocabulary and pronunciation. Each of these four elements is assessed for the interview as a whole.

The total mark available for the oral interview is 20. In the examination, this is scaled to represent 25% of the marks for the PET as a whole.

MARKING SCALES

MARK BANDS	STRUCTURAL ACCURACY	VOCABULARY	PRONUNCIATION	TASK ACHIEVEMENT
'with ease' level 4–5	Some structural inaccuracies which do not impede understanding	Range of words adequate for PET-level situations; can make effective use of paraphrase if necessary	L1 accent present but individual sounds, rhythm and stress usually clear enough to be understood	Each task dealt with effectively
'coping' level 2–3	Utterances partially obscured by structural errors	Range of words limited but generally sufficient for intelligibility	L1 accent strong enough to interfere with comprehension occasionally	Some difficulties with certain tasks but overall ability to cope; able to elicit clarification when necessary
'inability' level 0–1	Large number of errors make utterances unintelligible	Too few words to make communication possible	L1 accent so strong that communication breaks down	Unable to deal with basic requirements of most tasks

It is clear from the Marking Scale that a faultless performance is not required to achieve top marks. Provided that the candidate has communicated effectively and appropriately, minor errors are disregarded. Such errors would be the occasional omission of the 's' for the third person singular in the present simple, or wrong word order, where this does not impair comprehensibility. However, gross tense errors, such as 'I am staying here since three months' would be penalised. As far as vocabulary is concerned, students will not be penalised for lack of any particular word, provided that they have the resources to explain what they mean. For example, they would not be expected to know 'rucksack', but should be able to say something like: 'It is a bag you use to carry things on your back when you go for a walk.' Naturally, no student at this level would be expected to pronounce English like a native speaker. The best candidates should be readily comprehensible, showing some knowledge of basic intonation and stress patterns. If candidates pronounce words so inaccurately that it is difficult to tell whether they are saying 'can' or 'can't', 'hungry' or 'angry', then the pronunciation is more or less unintelligible and will get fewer marks.

The Oral

FRAMEWORKS FOR CONDUCTING THE ORAL

UNIT 1   SHOPPING AND SERVICES

SECTION I

Tasks: Identifying oneself, giving information about things

Sub tasks: Spelling, numbers, responding to questions/information

Framework: (Where a pause is indicated, allow a few seconds, then prompt if no response is forthcoming.)

Teacher:
Please sit down. What's your name?

Can you tell me where you come from?

Can you spell that for me please?

(Write down and repeat)

I haven't heard of that.   *Ah yes, I know . . . . I was*
Where is it?   *there in . . . .*
And how long have you been learning English?

Why are you learning English? For you job, for fun or . . . ?

(React – continue conversation if time allows.)
Thank you.

Time: About two minutes.

SECTION I   PAIRWORK OPTION

Tasks: Identifying oneself, giving information about people/things, asking direct questions

Sub tasks: Spelling, numbers, responding to questions/information

Frameworks for conducting the Oral

Framework: Teacher:
Please sit down.
What are your names?

Do you know each other?

(if 'yes') (if 'no')
Imagine/pretend you don't *Can you find out some*
know each other and find *information about each*
out some information *other?*
about each other.

The students' exchange should consist of 4 or 5 turns each. If necessary prompt to elicit information on home town, schools, jobs, family etc. Select a suitable word for spelling from each student and ask for it at the end of the exchange.
e.g. *Miki, you said you came from Osaka – how do you spell that?*
(Thank the students and move on to Section II.)

Time: About two or three minutes.

SECTION II

Tasks: Making a complaint, describing and explaining

Framework: Teacher (slowly):
Now I am going to describe a situation to you.

Last week you bought an alarm clock. It has stopped working so you have brought it back to the shop.
(Ask student to look at picture 1A in the colour section.)
I am the shop assistant. Explain to me what has happened.

Just think for a few seconds.
(Pause)
Is that all right?
Shall I repeat it?

(briskly) *Good morning sir/madam, can I help you?*

And when exactly did you buy it?

Have you dropped it by any chance?

The Oral

       Have you still got your receipt?

       If you wait a few minutes I'll call the manager.

       Thank you.

Time: About two minutes.

SECTION II   PAIRWORK OPTION

Tasks: Making a complaint, describing and explaining

Framework: Teacher (slowly):
Now I am going to describe a situation to you.

You are in a shop.
(Ask students to look at picture 1A in the colour section.)
(to Student A) *You are the customer. You bought an alarm clock last week and it has since stopped working so you have brought it back to the shop.*
(to Student B) *You are the shop assistant. You ask the customer whether you can help her/him.*

Just think for a few seconds. (Pause)
Is that all right?
Shall I repeat it? Are you ready?
Right, B, you begin.

Thank you.

Time: About two or three minutes.

SECTION III

Tasks: Identifying other people, discussing what others are doing, saying where things are

Framework: Teacher:
Look at this photograph (point to photo 1B in the colour section) *and tell me about it.*
(Prompts rather than direct questions should be used if necessary.)
Information should include:
– setting and location
– people (activities, clothes, goods on sale)

Time: Sections III and IV should take about four minutes together.

SECTION III   PAIRWORK OPTION

Tasks: Identifying other people, discussing what others are doing, saying where things are

Framework: Teacher:
(to Student A) *Look at this photograph.*
(point to photo 1B in the colour section)
(to Student B) *Look at this photograph.*
(point to photo C in the colour section)
Don't look at each other's photos.
Now I want you to talk about your photos.
Are they the same or different?
(Prompts rather than direct questions should be used if necessary. At the end let them study each other's photographs for a few moments.)

Time: Sections III and IV should take about four minutes together.

SECTION IV

Tasks: Talking about one's likes and dislikes, experiences, habits

Framework: Teacher:
(using either/both photo(s) 1B or/and 1C)
What kind of shop do you like?
Where do you usually shop?
Do you have a favourite kind of shop?
Do you prefer street markets to ordinary shops?

Time: Sections III and IV should take about four minutes together.

SECTION IV   PAIRWORK OPTION

Tasks: Talking about one's likes and dislikes, experiences, habits

Framework: Teacher (to both students):
Ask each other about shopping preferences.
Find out if your partner likes shopping in a market or an ordinary shop and why.

Time: Sections III and IV should take about four minutes together.

The Oral

UNIT 2   HEALTH AND MEDICINE

SECTION I

Tasks: Identifying oneself, giving information about things

Sub tasks: Spelling, numbers, responding to questions/information

Framework: (Where a pause is indicated, allow a few seconds, then prompt if no response is forthcoming.)

Teacher:
Please sit down. What's your name?

Where are you studying? Which school/college do you go to?

I haven't heard of that.
Can you spell the name for me please?

And how long have you been studying there?

(React – continue conversation if time allows.)
Thank you.

Time: About two minutes.

SECTION I   PAIRWORK OPTION

Tasks: Identifying oneself, giving information about people/things, asking direct questions

Sub tasks: Spelling, numbers, responding to questions/information

Framework: Teacher:
Please sit down.
What are your names?

Do you know each other?

(if 'yes')
Imagine/pretend you don't know each other and find out some information about each other.

(if 'no')
Can you find out some information about each other?

Frameworks for conducting the Oral

The students' exchange should consist of about 4 or 5 turns each. If necessary prompt to elicit information on home town, schools, jobs, family etc.
Select a suitable word for spelling from each student and ask for it at the end of the exchange.
e.g. *Stefan, you said your surname was Pfestorf – how do you spell that?*

(Thank the students and move on to Section II.)

Time: About two or three minutes.

SECTION II

Tasks: Asking for help, explaining, describing

Framework: Teacher (slowly):
You are on holiday in Britain. You don't feel very well.
(Ask student to look at photo 2A in the colour section.)
You have decided to ask for help at the chemist's.
I am the chemist. Ask me for help.

Just think for a few seconds.
(Pause)
Is that all right?
Shall I repeat it?
....
(briskly) *Next please – can I help you?*
....
When did it begin to/Where does it hurt?
....
Have you tried ....
.... ?

Time: About two minutes.

SECTION II PAIRWORK OPTION

Tasks: Asking for help, explaining, describing

Framework: Teacher (slowly):
You are on holiday in Britain. Neither of you feels well.
Discuss what you should do to get help.

25

The Oral

Just think for a few seconds.
(Pause)
Is that all right?
Shall I repeat it? Are you ready?
Right, . . . you begin.

Thank you.

Time: About two or three minutes.

SECTION III

Tasks: Identifying other people, discussing and describing what others are doing

Framework: Teacher:
Look at these photographs (point to photos 2B and 2C) *and tell me about them.*
(Prompts rather than direct questions should be used if necessary.)
What is happening in each one?
Information should include:
– people's activities, clothing
– setting/environment

Time: Sections III and IV should take about four minutes together.

SECTION III   PAIRWORK OPTION

Tasks: Identifying other people, discussing and describing what others are doing

Framework: Teacher:
(to Student A) *Look at this photograph.*
(point to photo 2B in the colour section)
(to Student B) *Look at this photograph.*
(point to photo 2C in the colour section)
Don't look at each other's photos.
Now I want you to find out about each other's photos.
(Prompts rather than direct questions should be used if necessary. At the end let them study the pictures together for a few moments.)

Time: Sections III and IV should take about four minutes together.

Frameworks for conducting the Oral

SECTION IV

Tasks: Talking about one's likes and dislikes, experiences, habits

Framework: Teacher:
(using photo 2B if necessary)
What kind of things do you like to do to keep fit and healthy?
Do you do any of the activities you can see people doing in this photo?
Are you careful over what you eat?

Time: Sections III and IV should take about four minutes together.

SECTION IV PAIRWORK OPTION

Tasks: Talking about one's likes and dislikes, experiences, habits

Framework: Teacher (to both students):
I want you to find out what your partner does to keep fit and healthy. Do you take any exercise? Do you take care not to eat too much?

Time: Sections III and IV should take about four minutes together.

The Oral

UNIT 3 TRAVEL AND TOURISM

SECTION I

Tasks: Identifying oneself, giving information about things

Sub tasks: Spelling, numbers, responding to questions/information

Framework: (Where a pause is indicated, allow a few seconds, then prompt if no response is forthcoming.)
Teacher:
Please sit down. What's your name?

Can you tell me how old you are?

Where do you come from?

(if local)
So this is your home town. Whereabouts do you live?

(if another place)
That's quite near/a long way from here.

Can you spell that, please?

(Pause . . . prompt)
What's the name of your street?

(Write down and repeat)

I don't know where that is.

I think I know where that is.

Can you spell that please?

How did you get here today?

Are you learning English for your job, or for fun or . . . ?

(React – continue conversation if time allows.)
Thank you.

Time: About two minutes.

SECTION I   PAIRWORK OPTION

Tasks: Identifying oneself, giving information about people/things, asking direct questions

Sub tasks: Spelling, numbers, responding to questions/information

Framework: Teacher:
Please sit down.
What are your names?

Frameworks for conducting the Oral

Do you know each other?

(if 'yes') | (if 'no')
Imagine/pretend you don't know each other and find out some information about each other. | *Find out some information about each other.*

The students' exchange should consist of about 4 or 5 turns each. If necessary prompt to elicit information on home town, schools, jobs, family etc.
Select a suitable word for spelling from each student and ask for it at the end of the exchange.
e.g. *Riitaa, you said you came from Helsinki – how do you spell that?*

(Thank the students and move on to Section II.)

Time: About two or three minutes.

SECTION II

Tasks: Inviting, describing, explaining

Framework: Teacher (slowly):
Now I am going to describe a situation to you. You want to go on a bus tour of England and you want me to come with you.
(Ask student to look at leaflet 3A)
Tell me what we can see and try to persuade me to come with you.
Just think for a few seconds.
(Pause)
Is that all right?
Shall I repeat it?

Please begin.

Where exactly will we stop?

I've never been there –

That sounds interesting, is it very expensive?

Let's book our tickets then, shall we?

Time: About two minutes.

The Oral

SECTION II   PAIRWORK OPTION

Tasks: Inviting, describing, explaining, asking for clarification

Framework: Teacher (slowly):
Now I am going to describe a situation to you.
(To Student A) You want to go on a bus tour of England and you want . . . (Student B) to come with you.
(Indicate leaflet 3A to Student A)
Tell her/him what you can see and try to persuade her/him to come with you.
Just think for a few seconds.
(To Student B) You have to listen to . . . (Student A) and ask her/him for more information. You're rather busy, but perhaps you can go if the tour is really good.
(Pause)
(To both students) Is that all right?
Shall I repeat it?

....

Please begin.

....

Time: About two or three minutes.

SECTION III

Tasks: Identifying other people; discussing what others are doing; saying where things are

Framework: Teacher:
Look at this photograph (point to photo 3B) *and tell me about it.*
(Prompts rather than direct questions should be used if necessary.)
Information should include:
– setting
– people (characteristics, clothes, location, differences)
– activities

Time: Sections III and IV should take about four minutes together.

SECTION III   PAIRWORK OPTION

Tasks: Identifying other people; discussing what others are doing; saying where things are

Frameworks for conducting the Oral

Framework: Teacher:
(To Student A) *Look at this photograph.*
(point to photo 3B)
(To Student B) *Look at this photograph.*
(point to photo 3C)
Don't look at each other's pictures.
Now I want you to talk about your pictures.
Are they the same or different?
(Prompts rather than direct questions should be used if necessary. At the end let them study each other's photographs for a few moments.)

Time: Sections III and IV should take about four minutes together.

SECTION IV

Tasks: Talking about one's likes and dislikes, experiences, habits

Framework: Teacher:
Do you like travelling by bus?

Why/Why not?
What do you think is the best way to travel?
Why?

Time: Sections III and IV should take about four minutes together.

SECTION IV   PAIRWORK OPTION

Tasks: Talking about one's likes and dislikes, experiences, habits

Framework: Teacher:
(to both students)
Ask each other about travelling.
Find out how your partner likes to travel and why.

Time: Sections III and IV should take about four minutes together.

The Oral

UNIT 4   FAMILY, EDUCATION AND SOCIETY

SECTION I

Tasks: Identifying oneself, giving information about things

Sub tasks: Spelling, numbers, responding to questions/information

Framework: (Where a pause is indicated, allow a few seconds, then prompt if no response is forthcoming.)
Teacher:
Please sit down. What's your name?

Can you tell me your address?

Could you spell your street for me, please?

And where do you come from?

I've never been there.   *I was there in 19......*

(Pause . . . prompt)   (Pause . . . prompt)
What is it like?   *Has it changed much?*

Are you learning English for your job, or for fun or . . . ?

(React – continue conversation if time allows.)
Thank you.

Time: About two minutes.

SECTION I   PAIRWORK OPTION

Tasks: Identifying oneself, giving information about people/things, asking direct questions

Sub tasks: Spelling, numbers, responding to questions/information

32

Framework: Teacher:
Please sit down.
What are your names?

Do you know each other?

(if 'yes')
Imagine/pretend you don't know each other and find out some information about each other.

(if 'no')
Find out some information about each other.

The students' exchange should consist of about 4 or 5 turns each. If necessary prompt to elicit information on home town, schools, jobs, family etc.
Select a suitable word for spelling from each student and ask for it at the end of the exchange.
e.g. *Bernard, you said you're at the Chester Institute how do you spell Chester?*

(Thank the students and move on to Section II.)

Time: About two or three minutes.

SECTION II

Tasks: Asking for information, describing needs, asking for clarification

Framework: Teacher (slowly):
Now I am going to describe a situation to you.
You want to take extra English classes. You have come to a language school to find out what it offers.
Here are some of the things you may need to know.
(Ask student to look at list 4A.)
I am the receptionist at the school. Ask me about it.
Just think for a few seconds.
(Pause)
Is that all right?
Shall I repeat it?

Good afternoon, can I help you?

What exactly do you need to know?

(Teacher may refer to advertisement 4B, or invent information, as preferred.)

Time: About two minutes.

The Oral

SECTION II PAIRWORK OPTION

Tasks: Asking for information, describing needs, asking for clarification

Framework: Teacher (slowly):
Now I am going to describe a situation to you.
(to Student A) *You want to take extra English classes. You have come to a language school to find out what it offers. Here are some of the things you may need to know.*
(Ask student to look at list 4A.)
You are going to ask the receptionist about them.
(to Student B) *You are the receptionist at the school. Here is some information about your school.* (Indicate advertisement 4B.)
You have to answer your partner's questions.
Just think for a few seconds.
(Pause)
Is that all right?
Shall I repeat it?

Teacher (to Student B):
Please begin.

Time: About two minutes.

SECTION III

Tasks: Identifying other people; discussing relationships

Framework: Teacher:
Look at this photograph (point to photo 4C) *and tell me about it.*
(Prompts rather than direct questions should be used if necessary.)
Information should include:
– setting
– people (characteristics, clothes, location, differences)

Time: Sections III and IV should take about four minutes together.

SECTION III PAIRWORK OPTION

Tasks: Identifying other people; discussing relationships

Frameworks for conducting the Oral

Framework: Teacher:
(to student A) *Look at this photograph*
(point to photo 4C)
(to Student B) *Look at this photograph*
(point to photo 4D)
Don't look at each other's pictures.
Now I want you to talk about your pictures.
Are they the same or different?
(Prompts rather than direct questions should be used if necessary. At the end let them study each other's photographs for a few moments.)

Time: Sections III and IV should take about four minutes together.

SECTION IV

Tasks: Talking about families, feelings, habits

Framework: Teacher:
Do you ever take family photographs?

Why/Why not?

Do you often see your grandparents/cousins etc?

Time: Sections III and IV should take about four minutes together.

SECTION IV   PAIRWORK OPTION

Tasks: Talking about families, feelings, habits

Framework: Teacher:
(to both students)
Ask each other about your families.
Find out how often your partner sees all her/his relatives.

Time: Sections III and IV should take about four minutes together.

The Oral

UNIT 5 PET PRACTICE TEST PAPER

SECTION I

Tasks: Identifying oneself, giving information about things

Sub tasks: Spelling, numbers, responding to questions/information

Framework: (Where a pause is indicated, allow a few seconds, then prompt if no response is forthcoming.)

Teacher:
Please sit down. What's your name?

Where do you come from?

Can you spell it for me, please?

How long have you been learning English?

Why are you learning it?

(React – continue conversation if time allows.)
Thank you.

Time: About two minutes.

SECTION II

Tasks: Asking for information, describing needs, asking for clarification

Framework: Teacher (slowly):
Now I am going to describe a situation to you.
You want to take a holiday in the USA. You have come to a travel agent's to get some information.
Here is a picture to give you some ideas.
(Ask student to look at photomontage 5A.)
Tell me about the sort of places you'd like to visit and ask me about getting there.
Just think for a few seconds.
(Pause)
Is that all right?
Shall I repeat it?

Frameworks for conducting the Oral

Good afternoon, can I help you?

What sort of areas would you like to visit?

(Teacher may improvise travel information, as necessary.)

Time: About two minutes.

SECTION III

Tasks: Describing places, people; making guesses

Framework: Teacher:
Look at this plan (point to plan and elevation 5B).
Describe this house for me.
What sort of people do you think live here?
(Prompts rather than direct questions should be used if necessary.)
e.g. *I suppose it might be a holiday home.*
Information should include:
– description of house
– suppositions about people

Time: Sections III and IV should take about four minutes together.

SECTION IV

Tasks: Talking about one's home, likes and dislikes

Framework: Teacher:
Is this at all like your own house?

Why/Why not?

What sort of place would you most like to live in?

Time: Sections III and IV should take about four minutes together.

Answer keys

UNIT 1   SHOPPING AND SERVICES

QUESTION 1   One mark for each correct answer

1. Box 4   2. Box 1   3. Box 4   4. Box 2   5. Box 3

QUESTION 2   One mark for each correct answer

1. B   2. A   3. D   4. A   5. D   6. C   7. B   8. A
9. B   10. A

QUESTION 3   One mark for each correct answer

1. H or D   2. A   3. F   4. C   5. E

QUESTION 4   Half a mark for each correct answer

1. N   2. Y   3. Y   4. N   5. Y   6. Y   7. N   8. N
9. N   10. Y

QUESTION 5   7 marks (1 mark each for 1, 2 and 5; 2 marks each for 3 and 4)

1. Box 3   2. Box 2
3. (It was a good thing) because the first film had been/was lost in the post/at least not all the films were lost in the post.
4. . . . it would be better/best to pay/give her some money and avoid going/not go to court.
5. C

QUESTION 6   One mark for each correct answer

1. . . . the shop assistant whether/whether the shop assistant/she/they had a pale blue sweater.
2. . . . showed me was too small.
3. . . . the red sweater cost?' I asked.
4. . . . was not as expensive as the red sweater/cheaper than the red sweater.
5. . . . buy either (one).

QUESTION 7   Total 10 marks. Half a mark for each appropriate and correct completion of questions 1–9a; up to 2 marks each (1 for language and 1 for content) for questions 10 and 11. See page 40.

QUESTION 8   Total 10 marks (5 for language and 5 for content). See page 41.

Unit 1 Shopping and services

QUESTION 9   One mark for each correct answer

1. Box 3   2. Box 2   3. Box 4   4. Box 1   5. Box 2   6. Box 2
7. Box 1

QUESTION 10   One mark for each correct answer

1. Box 1   2. Box 2   3. Box 3   4. Box 4   5. Box 2   6. Box 3

QUESTION 11   One mark each for 1, 3, 4, 5, 8 and 9; half a mark each for 2, 6, 7 and 10

1. boots   2. 3/three   3. trousers   4. shirts   5. sweaters
6. hat   7. 2/two   8. towels   9. shorts   10. bag

QUESTION 12   Half a mark for each correct answer

1. No   2. No   3. No   4. Yes   5. Yes   6. Yes

Answer keys

Sample student answer to Question 7

SHOPPING BY POST

Join this special club for the best clothes at affordable prices.
Just fill in this form and post it today!

1. MR   MRS   (MS)
2. SURNAME   MORINAGA
3. INITIALS   S.M
4. ADDRESS   29-3-707 yamada-minami
   Suita City OSAKA, 〒.565 JAPAN

5. PHONE NO (06) 878-4530
6. AGE   20
7. DO YOU HAVE A BANK ACCOUNT?   (YES)/NO
7a. NAME OF BANK   MIDLAND BANK, ~~kantei~~, MITSUI GINKŌ
8. ARE YOU A STUDENT?   (YES)/NO
8a. NAME OF SCHOOL OR COLLEGE   CHICHESTER SCHOOL OF ENGLISH
9. ARE YOU EMPLOYED?   YES/(NO)
9a. NAME OF COMPANY

10. WHAT SORT OF CLOTHES DO YOU LIKE TO WEAR?
    SOMETIME JEANS, CASUAL BUT SOME TIME SMARTRY
    ANY KIND OF CLOTHES EXCEPT SHABBY
    and OLD STILE   DEPEND ON MY FEELING

11. DO YOU HAVE ANY SPECIAL NEEDS?
    (eg unusual size, for sport, dancing, holiday etc)
    Sports → SKY, TENNIS, SWIMMING
    Dance → BALET, DISCO'S DANCE
    Holiday → TRAVEL

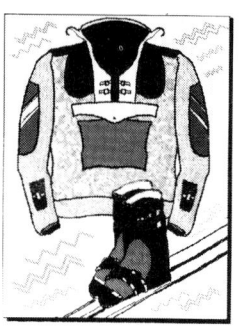

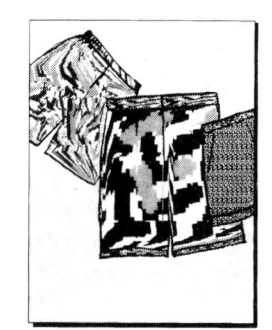

Suggested mark: $\frac{1}{2}+\frac{1}{2}+\frac{1}{2}+\frac{1}{2}+\frac{1}{2}+\frac{1}{2}+\frac{1}{2}+\frac{1}{2}+\frac{1}{2}+\frac{1}{2}+\frac{1}{2}+\frac{1}{2}+1+1=8$

Unit 1 Shopping and services

Sample student answer to Question 8

Dear ...Mary...............
I think you will be interested to know what Ingsdon is like. There is nothing to worry about ^becoming bored ~~so~~ because there is your favorite cinema and theatre. There **are** also really good shopping centre where you can buy everything you need, and if you want buy something fresh you would be able to buy in the Market square. In addition, this town has quite a lot of nature such as gardens and park. Furthermore near this there is a Concert hall ~~...~~ and library as well. This town is ~~busy~~ becuase of there is a college. But I must say this town ~~a~~ could be called ^quiet London.
Any way I think you will ^little like this town.

Suggested mark: 2+4=6

TRANSCRIPT

UNIT 1   SHOPPING AND SERVICES

Preliminary English Test Listening Test

There are four questions: numbers 9, 10, 11 and 12. Now, look at the instructions for Question 9 only.

As you can see, this question has seven parts, each with four pictures. For each part there will be a short recording, which you will hear twice. You must put a tick in the box under the picture you think is the most suitable.

Answer keys

Before we start, here is an example:

Woman: Postman's here, Tom, there are two letters and a packet for you.

[Pause . . . Repeat as above . . . Pause.]

The woman is telling Tom that the postman has brought a packet and two letters. So the fourth picture is the most suitable and the tick has been put in the box under that picture.

Now we are ready to start. Here is a short recording for the first four pictures. Don't forget to put a tick in one of the boxes!

Listen carefully.

1. Woman 1:   Where do I go to pay this bill please?
    Woman 2:   You want the desk over there – the one where the young man is.
    [Pause . . . Repeat . . . Pause.]

2. Man: I'd like these trousers cleaned please and there's a hole in one of the knees. Can you do anything about that?
    Woman: Yes, we can mend that before cleaning. Name, please?
    [Pause . . . Repeat . . . Pause.]

3. Man: I've come to clean the windows.
    Woman: Can you just do the upstairs please – the downstairs ones don't need doing.
    [Pause . . . Repeat . . . Pause.]

4. Woman 1:   Can I make an appointment to have my hair cut please?
    Woman 2:   With anyone in particular?
    Woman 1:   I usually have the nice young girl – I can't remember her name . . .
    [Pause . . . Repeat . . . Pause.]

5. Man: Can I have two loaves, please?
    Woman: Large or small?
    Man: One of each please.
    [Pause . . . Repeat . . . Pause.]

6. Man: Have you any shoes which need repairing?
    Woman: My shoes are OK, but these boots need to have the part round the top fixed, it seems to have come loose.
    [Pause . . . Repeat . . . Pause.]

Unit 1 Shopping and services

7. Man: Do you want the washing-machine beside the sink?
   Woman: I think it'd be best to have it there, otherwise we'll have to run pipes round the cupboard in the corner, won't we?
   Man: Oh, yes, of course.
   [Pause . . . Repeat . . . Pause.]

That is the end of Question 9.

You now have half a minute to check your answers. We will tell you when Question 10 begins.

Now look at Question 10. *As you can see, this time there are six parts. Imagine that you are with a party of tourists in a coach. Your guide has given you a map of Brimston city centre. Listen to what he says and put a tick in the right box – one tick for each of the six parts. You must do this while you are listening because the speaker will not stop and repeat each part separately. At the end, after all six parts are finished, the whole recording will be repeated.*

[Pause] . . . *Now we're ready to start. Listen carefully.*

Courier: Right – if I could have everyone's attention please? Is the bus full? No empty seats?
Voices: No . . . no. We're all here.
Courier: Thank you – so if you could just bear with me for a minute. Now I know you've all enjoyed our boat trip. As I told you earlier, this afternoon is our shopping afternoon. If you look on the back page of your tour programme, you'll see a little map of Brimston city centre, with the names of some of the shops marked. As you won't have too much time, I'm just going to explain to you what they sell.
   First of all there's Barrs'. It's a very good place for leather goods – bags and gloves and so on, rather than shoes or boots, I mean. Not cheap, but some beautiful things often with really unusual patterns on them, which you can't find anywhere else.
   Opposite Barrs' there's Crampling and Co. They have excellent hand-sewn clothes for women. Again, not cheap, but all locally made, and really pretty. Next to them there's Greens'. Now that's a marvellous place for books – as long as you don't want new ones! They've got old books on just about every subject anyone has ever written about, from aeroplanes to zebras, but fact only – so none of your favourite old detective or love stories I'm afraid. But we can all afford a book from Greens', because their prices are very reasonable.
   Now I know some of you are sports enthusiasts, so if you want to find some good sportswear at very cheap prices, try Garretts'. They don't sell shoes, which means no football boots, but a great many shirts, shorts, running suits, etc. And not at all expensive.

Answer keys

Opposite Garretts' there's a travel agency, where you can cash travellers' cheques if you need to. Then there's a tea shop, which has very good cakes, and then there's Brimston Craft Centre. They sell traditional local sweets, as well as hand-made wooden chairs, tables and so on which you can order to be sent to your home address.

And the last place of particular interest to tourists is Drovers'. This is your chance to buy some unusual food presents: they sell a truly amazing variety of cheeses, from all over the country, made with goats' and sheep's milk besides cows'. By the way, if you do buy one of the strong-smelling ones, ask them to double wrap it for you. That extra covering of plastic will make sure the bus still smells sweet on our way home!

Now we'll be in Brimston in about 20 minutes. Don't hesitate to ask me if there's anything else you want to know . . . FADE

[Pause] . . . *Now listen again.*

[Repeat recording.]

You now have a minute to check your answers. We will tell you when the next question begins.

Now look at Question 11. *You will hear a recording of a radio programme about activity holidays. You must listen to it and write the correct information in the spaces in your answer book. You don't need to write very much, only a number or a few words. At the end, the recording will be repeated.*

[Pause] . . . *Now we're ready to start. Listen carefully.*

Presenter: . . . now for those of you planning to join one of the activity holidays which we've been discussing in this week's programme, Christine is here with some advice.

Woman: Hello, yes, I've found it very helpful to plan what to take on these activity weekends and it's essential you take the right things with you otherwise you could spoil your holiday. For those of you planning a weekend hill walking and climbing: strong boots are a must and at least three pairs of thick socks. Waterproof trousers and jacket are also a good idea but if you haven't got those, then a warm pair of trousers and a thick jacket. You'll need cotton shirts and at least two sweaters. If you've got room, take a woollen hat and gloves as it can really get cold at times. Wrap up warm and you'll have a great time!

Now from one extreme to the other – those of you flying off for a deep-sea diving weekend in the Mediterranean! Obviously you'll hire your equipment when you get there but make sure you have at least two swimsuits with you – there's nothing worse

Visual material for the Oral

1A

1B

Visual material for the Oral

1C

2A

II

Visual material for the Oral

2B

2C

Visual material for the Oral

3A

SOUTH OF ENGLAND ONE DAY TOUR

DEPART LONDON 7.30 a.m.
First stop: *Salisbury*

Second stop: *lunch at country hotel in New Forest (one of England's oldest National Parks)*

Third stop: *Bournemouth for shopping (or just relax by the sea)*

RETURN LONDON 7.30 p.m.
£12.00 including lunch

3B

Visual material for the Oral

3C

Visual material for the Oral

4A

student numbers?
cost?
times of classes?
conversation only?
special interest lessons?

4B

WESSEX LANGUAGE SCHOOL

Small classes – maximum 10 per class

19.30 – 21.00 Mon, Tues, Wed, Thurs

English for Scientists 18.00 – 19.00 Tues & Wed

Phone 82 8340

We're not the cheapest – but we are the best!

Visual material for the Oral

4C

4D

Visual material for the Oral

5A

5B

VIII

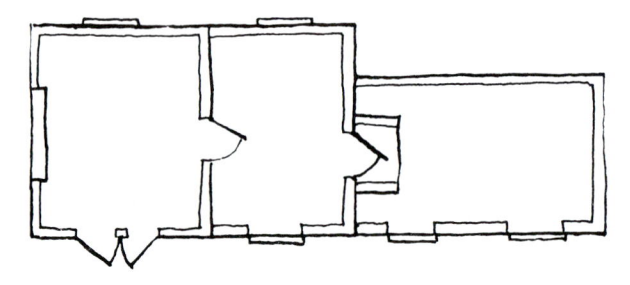

Unit 1 Shopping and services

than waiting around in a wet bathing costume. You'll need plenty of large towels, at least two pairs of shorts, a pair of light shoes, a cotton sweater as it can get chilly in the evenings and finally a lightweight bag that you can pack all your equipment into before you set off each morning. Last year when I went . . .
. . .

[Pause] . . . *Now listen again.*

[Repeat recording.]

You now have a minute to check your answers. We will tell you when the next question begins.

Now look at Question 12. *You will hear a husband and wife discussing whether to buy someone a present. As you can see there are six statements. Listen to the recording and decide if you agree with each statement. If you agree, put a tick in the box under 'Yes'. If you do not agree, put a tick in the box under 'No'. At the end, the recording will be repeated.*

[Pause] . . . *Listen carefully.*
[This is a friendly discussion.]

Wife: I was wondering what we could give Stephanie?

Husband: You mean when she moves into her new house? Yes, that's a nice idea. What about a book?

Wife: She won't thank us for that – she'll be so busy painting and arranging things, she won't want to read.

Husband: She'll want to sit down sometimes! OK, so what do you suggest? A paintbrush?

Wife: Of course not! But we should give her something . . . well . . . something . . . like some cups or glasses, something like that.

Husband: You mean something useful – and boring! I suppose you think a saucepan or a rubbish bin would be more suitable?

Wife: Don't be silly. You know what I mean – we ought to give her something for the house. Yes, useful if you like, but nice as well.

Husband: Well I think some really expensive soap would be the thing, something to help her feel better after a hard day moving furniture.

45

Answer keys

Wife: That's much better – perhaps we could find a pretty towel to give with it – then she'd have something that would last longer.

Husband: Not a bad idea! Can you get them tomorrow?

Wife: I think you should get them. She's your sister, after all. And I've got two big meetings tomorrow, I just won't have enough time.

Husband: But I won't know what to choose! What smell? What colour?

Wife: I'm sure you'll find something if you try.

Husband: Oh dear. I wish I hadn't said it was a good idea! . . . FADE

[Pause] . . . *Now listen again.*

[Repeat recording.]

You now have a minute to check your answers.

That is the end of the test.

UNIT 2 HEALTH AND MEDICINE

QUESTION 1 One mark for each correct answer

1. Box 4   2. Box 4   3. Box 4   4. Box 1   5. Box 3

QUESTION 2 One mark for each correct answer

1. A   2. D   3. C   4. A   5. B   6. D   7. C   8. A
9. A   10. B

QUESTION 3 One mark for each correct answer

1. B   2. A or B   3. D   4. C   5. F   6. E

QUESTION 4 Half a mark for each correct answer

1. Y   2. N   3. Y   4. N   5. N   6. N   7. Y   8. N

QUESTION 5 7 marks (1 mark each for 1, 2 and 5; 2 marks each for 3 and 4)

1. Box 3   2. Box 3
3. . . . they avoid putting all their weight on their feet.
4. . . . You can damage muscles that aren't used to working.
5. C

QUESTION 6 One mark for each correct answer

1. . . . well enough to go to work.
2. . . . examined him.
3. . . . work too hard,' his doctor told him.
4. . . . better take/have a holiday,' the doctor continued.
5. . . . you rest you really will be ill!'

QUESTION 7 Total 10 marks

lines 1–4   half a mark for each appropriate and correct completion
line 5   up to 2 marks
line 6   up to 3 marks
line 7   up to 2 marks
signature   half a mark
date   half a mark   See page 48.

QUESTION 8 Total 10 marks   See page 49.

QUESTION 9 One mark for each correct answer

1. Box 1   2. Box 3   3. Box 2   4. Box 1   5. Box 3
6. Box 4   7. Box 1

QUESTION 10 One mark for each correct answer

1. Box 1   2. Box 2   3. Box 2   4. Box 4   5. Box 2   6. Box 2

47

Answer keys

QUESTION 11   One mark each for 1, 2, 3 and 6; 2 marks each for 4 and 5

1. DARCY   2. J H   3. 1–7–(19)15   4. 3 High Street, Barton
5. broken left thumb   6. fall/fell (while shopping)

QUESTION 12   Half a mark for each correct answer

1. Yes   2. Yes   3. No   4. No   5. No   6. No

Sample student answer to Question 7

SUNSPOT HOLIDAYS
INSURANCE CLAIM FORM

full name AYTEN ÇALIK   MR/MRS/MISS/MS

address Elma Sitesi
Meltep Sok.
Olcay blk daire 26
80600 Zincirlikuyu Istanbul TURKEY

date of birth 13.03.1963

occupation Geologist

Where did the accident happen? Please give the exact place.
In Chichester – Adelaid Road

Describe how you were hurt as clearly as possible please.
When I was driving to the school, a cat ran out in front of my car and I had to stop so suddenly that the car behind crashed into me.

How long did you spend in hospital? a couple of weeks

SIGNED 13 December 1989

DATE [signature]

Suggested mark: $\frac{1}{2}+\frac{1}{2}+\frac{1}{2}+\frac{1}{2}+1+0+2+\frac{1}{2}+\frac{1}{2}=6$

Sample student answer to Question 8

Dear Anne,

Thanks for the postcard. I'm glad everything's well with you. I myself am feeling well. But, I shoul be carefully when I chose my food. Because I have to change my eating habits in order to improve my health. I can eat green salad, fresh fruits, as much as I want. Also I can drink tea. Every day I shoul eat chicken, and egg or fish and beans or cheese. Any two of them should be eaten.

I am allowed to eat rice, pasta, potatoes. unless I don't eat them so much.

I must cut down on eating sugar, butter and drinking coffe too.

Actually, it doesn't easy for me to cut down on drinking coffe. As you know, I like drinking coffee but I shoul obey to doctor's advice. This is for my healty.

What about you? I hope you're very well.

I'm looking forward to hearing from you as soon as possible.

     All my best wishes,
     yours,
     Ayten

Suggested mark: 3+4=7

TRANSCRIPT

UNIT 2   HEALTH AND MEDICINE

Preliminary English Test Listening Test

There are four questions: numbers 9, 10, 11 and 12. Now, look at the instructions for Question 9 only.

As you can see, this question has seven parts, each with four pictures. For each part there will be a short recording, which you will hear twice. You must put a tick in the box under the picture you think is the most suitable.

Before we start, here is an example:

Answer keys

Woman: Oh, you haven't finished your medicine. You've only drunk half of it!

[Pause . . . Repeat . . . Pause.]

The woman is saying that only half the medicine has been drunk. So the first picture is the most suitable and the tick has been put in the box under that picture.

Now we are ready to start. Here is a short recording for the first four pictures. Don't forget to put a tick in one of the boxes!

Listen carefully.

1. Woman: What's the matter? Have you hurt your neck?
   Man: No, it's my shoulder – I walked into a door!
   [Pause . . . Repeat . . . Pause.]

2. Man: Excuse me, could you tell me how to get to the children's ward please?
   Woman: Yes, at the end of this passage, turn left and it's the third door on the right.
   [Pause . . . Repeat . . . Pause.]

3. Woman: Health Centre, can I help you?
   Man: Can I make an appointment please?
   Woman: Which department do you want? Doctor, dentist, nurse or physio?
   Man: It's to have a tooth out.
   [Pause . . . Repeat . . . Pause.]

4. Woman: I think I must be ill, my chin's covered in spots!
   [Pause . . . Repeat . . . Pause.]

5. Woman: Emergency – which service please?
   Man: Ambulance please – a woman has fallen over in the High Street – she's lying on the pavement, I think she's unconscious . . .
   [Pause . . . Repeat . . . Pause.]

6. Woman: I'm afraid only two visitors are allowed to visit a patient.
   Man: Can't we take our baby in too? She's asleep.
   Woman: Yes, all right then.
   [Pause . . . Repeat . . . Pause.]

Unit 2 Health and medicine

7. Woman: Hold your arms out straight in front of you, keep your back straight and slowly bend your knees.
   [Pause . . . Repeat . . . Pause.]

That is the end of Question 9.

You now have half a minute to check your answers. We will tell you when Question 10 begins.

Now look at Question 10. *As you can see, this time there are six parts. Imagine that you are listening to one of the staff of the Health Farm. He is welcoming you and telling you what your weekend will be like. Put a tick in the right box – one tick for each of the six parts. You must do this while you are listening because the speaker will not stop and repeat each part separately. At the end, after all six parts are finished, the whole recording will be repeated.*

[Pause] . . . *Now we're ready to start. Listen carefully.*

Man: Welcome to Greenaways Health Farm and this 'Getting back to health' weekend. We're happy to see you all. We know that many of you have been seriously ill, but now you're on your way back to health. All the staff here are looking forward to showing you lots of ideas about healthy living which you can put into practice when you get back home. We hope you'll enjoy your weekend, but we also hope you won't be coming back again – because if you follow our advice you shouldn't need to! So – what are we going to do?
    First of all, in about ten minutes time, we'll be having a chance to meet each other and have a drink. One part of your new lifestyle will be getting used to drinking more tea and less coffee or other drinks which are not so good for your health, so we will encourage you to try different teas, made with flowers and fruit, to give you ideas of drinks that are safe but not boring.
    After that, there will be a talk, from six till seven, with plenty of opportunities for questions. This evening's talk will be about food – what we need to eat more of, and what we should avoid. That will probably make us all pretty hungry, but don't worry, supper is at a quarter past seven, so we shan't have long to wait. Some of you may be worried that you will have to give up all your favourite foods.
    Well, we hope that you will be pleasantly surprised by the meals over the weekend because they've been chosen to show that food can be good for you and taste good as well!
    After supper, you are welcome to take a walk in the gardens, or come to the library, where there will be a short film about new and safer medicines, starting at nine o'clock.
    Breakfast is at 8.30 each day, followed by practical classes. Tomorrow they'll be on cookery and exercise plans. After lunch there'll be a discussion on dealing with problems at work, how to avoid them and what we can do if they do arise.

Answer keys

> The cookery session is not in the kitchen, as you might expect, as that's not big enough, but in the large room next to the library, that's Room Four. We'll stay there to talk about exercise plans as well. Lunch, we hope, will be outside, if the weather is good enough.
> For the discussion, we'll divide into two groups.
> . . . FADE

[Pause] . . . *Now listen again.*

[Repeat recording.]

You now have a minute to check your answers. We will tell you when the next question begins.

Now look at Question 11. *You will hear a hospital clerk helping an old man with his admission card. You must listen to it and write the correct information in the spaces in your answer book. You don't need to write very much, only a number or a few words. At the end, the recording will be repeated.*

[Pause] . . . *Now we're ready to start. Listen carefully.*

Woman: Now Mr Darcy, I need to have this form filled in for the hospital records.

Man: Yes – but I haven't got my glasses – and I don't think I can –

Woman: That's all right, I'll do it, you just relax and tell me what to write, OK? Now, how do you spell your surname?

Man: D–A–R–C–Y.

Woman: Fine, and what're your initials?

Man: J.H.

Woman: J.H. Yes. And your date of birth?

Man: What?

Woman: When were you born?

Man: The first of July, nineteen-fifteen.

Woman: One, seven, fifteen. And your address?

Man: 3, High Street Barton.

Woman: Number 3?

Unit 2 Health and medicine

Man: Yes.

Woman: High, Street. B–A–R–T–O–N, right?

Man: Yes.

Woman: Fine. Now what's wrong with you, exactly?

Man: The doctor says I've broken my thumb.

Woman: Broken left thumb. And did he say how long you're to stay in hospital?

Man: He said a day or two, to make sure there's nothing else.

Woman: I see. Where did the injury happen? Were you at home?

Man: No, I was out shopping. I slipped and fell.

Woman: I see. Yes. So the cause of the injury was a fall. I expect that's why the doctor wants you to stay here for another day or so. Well, that's fine. I'll come and see you tomorrow, OK? Any questions?

Man: No, no. Thank you for your help. I'm quite comfy now.

Woman: Bye bye then . . . FADE

[Pause] . . . *Now listen again.*

[Repeat recording.]

You now have a minute to check your answers. We will tell you when the next question begins.

Now look at Question 12. *You will hear a conversation between a doctor and a patient. As you can see there are six statements. Listen to the recording and decide if you agree with each statement. If you agree, put a tick in the box under 'Yes'. If you do not agree, put a tick in the box under 'No'. At the end, the recording will be repeated.*

[Pause] . . . *Listen carefully.*
[The doctor remains polite but firm, whilst her patient is argumentative and only reluctantly cooperative at the end.]

Doctor: Come along in please, take a seat. Yes? It's Mrs Smith, isn't it? What can I do for you, Mrs Smith?

Answer keys

Woman: Well, it's this pain, Doctor, I saw you about it three weeks ago, I don't know whether you remember –

Doctor: Just a moment, let me look at your notes. Ah, yes, I remember, you had a pain in your . . .

Woman: In my arm and it's no better, that's why I've come back. In fact it's much worse than it was. I can't sleep. I can't lift anything –

Doctor: Now, I gave you a course of tablets, didn't I? Did you finish the course?

Woman: No, well, no, I didn't. They didn't make any difference you see. The pain was just as bad so I didn't think . . .

Doctor: Well, of course they won't help you unless you finish them. Taking just a few won't make any difference at all. I also gave you a diet sheet. I told you to eat less sugar and less salt. Did you follow my instructions?

Woman: Well, it's very difficult, Doctor, when you're cooking for a family. I keep forgetting. I couldn't stop putting salt and sugar in their food. So I thought if you could give me some new tablets which could clear up the pain more quickly –

Doctor: Look, Mrs Smith, there's no point in my giving you anything new. I'll write out another prescription for the same tablets and this time I want you to finish the course before –

Woman: But they didn't help me. I've just told you. I think I need stronger –

Doctor: And I want you to reduce the amount of salt and sugar you eat. Try drinking your tea and coffee without sugar, that won't affect your family will it? And come back and see me again in two weeks. All right, Mrs Smith?

Woman: Yes, Doctor. Doesn't seem to me I have any choice in the matter.

[Pause] . . . *Now listen again.*

[Repeat recording.]

You now have a minute to check your answers.

That is the end of the test.

UNIT 3   TRAVEL AND TOURISM

QUESTION 1   One mark for each correct answer

1. Box 2   2. Box 2   3. Box 2   4. Box 4   5. Box 2

QUESTION 2   One mark for each correct answer

1. A   2. B   3. C   4. D   5. B   6. A   7. C   8. C
9. A   10. C

QUESTION 3   One mark for each correct answer

1. E or B   2. F   3. A   4. D   5. F

QUESTION 4   Half a mark for each correct answer

1. N   2. Y   3. Y   4. Y   5. N   6. Y   7. N   8. Y
9. N   10. N

QUESTION 5   7 marks (1 mark each for 1, 2 and 5; 2 marks each for 3 and 4)

1. Box 4   2. Box 3
3. It/Hand baggage should only be put in official places.
   If flights are heavily booked there may be limits on the number of pieces (of hand baggage).
4. ... should only take one piece of hand luggage.
5. C

QUESTION 6   One mark for each correct answer
1. ... you arrive at the airport please ...
2. ... forget to check your ...
3. ... will check your passport ...
4. ... can buy tax free goods ...
5. ... will be some tax free goods on sale ...

QUESTION 7   Total 10 marks (8 for content and 2 for language). See page 56.

QUESTION 8   Total 10 marks. See page 57.

QUESTION 9   One mark for each correct answer

1. Box 3   2. Box 3   3. Box 3   4. Box 4   5. Box 2   6. Box 1
7. Box 4

QUESTION 10   One mark for each correct answer

1. Box 2   2. Box 2   3. Box 3   4. Box 4   5. Box 3   6. Box 3

Answer keys

QUESTION 11   Half a mark each for 4 and 6; 1 mark each for 1 and 3; 2 marks each for 2 and 5

1. sunset   2. West Gate   3. students   4. Box 3   5. Tuesday and Friday   6. Box 2

QUESTION 12   Half a mark for each correct answer

1. Yes   2. Yes   3. No   4. Yes   5. No

Sample student answer to Question 7

HOLIDAY REQUEST FORM

Please help your travel agent by filling in this form as fully as you can

Which countries are you interested in?
Do you want a touring holiday?
Do you want to camp?
Which month do you want to go away?
How long will your holiday be?
Are you travelling alone/with family and friends?
Any special requests?

I would like to go on holiday to Italy from the middle of August. I'll stay there for 1 month. In this holiday, I would like to sight seeing as much as I can. But I don't fancy doing this such as organised tour. I'd prefer to do myself. I'm going on this holiday with my friend. So, If you can I'd like to get a two-month-open-ticket, or varied of more than 1 month.

Suggested mark: 6 + 1 = 7

Unit 3 Travel and tourism

Sample student answer to Question 8

Dear Jane,

I'm so pleased you're going to visit my country. You'll need to know about various things so I'll try to give you as much information as I can. First of all the best time to go to Switzerland is in Summer. The cheapest way is by ferry and train; but the shortest one is by plane. It takes you only one and a half hour.

However the shops are open from 9 a.m. until 6.30 p.m., from monday till saturday. You'll find the same opening hours at the banks except on saturday because they are closed. Furthermore there are a lot of nice restaurants where you can find the typical Swiss "Rösti", and other national food. The famous part of Switzerland are the mountains. There are a lot of possibilities for climbing, if you are interested in it.

I am looking forward to seeing you soon and hope you will enjoy your holiday in my country.

Yours elisabeth

Suggested mark: 4+5=9

TRANSCRIPT

UNIT 3 TRAVEL AND TOURISM

Preliminary English Test Listening Test

There are four questions: numbers 9, 10, 11 and 12. Now, look at the instructions for Question 9 only.

As you can see, this question has seven parts, each with four pictures. For each part there will be a short recording, which you will hear twice. You must put a tick in the box under the picture you think is the most suitable.

Before we start, here is an example:

Man: Hurry up everyone, the coach is waiting . . .

[Pause . . . Repeat as above . . . Pause.]

The man says the coach is waiting. So the first picture is the most suitable and the tick has been put in the box under that picture.

Answer keys

Now we are ready to start. Here is a short recording for the first four pictures. Don't forget to put a tick in one of the boxes!

Listen carefully.

1. Woman: Will the driver of the car RGE 811B please move it immediately as it is in front of the hotel entrance.
   [Pause . . . Repeat . . . Pause.]

2. Woman: Two returns for the island ferry please – what time does it leave?
   Man: In about twenty minutes, at 10.30.
   [Pause . . . Repeat . . . Pause.]

3. Woman 1: Is there somewhere we could try local food?
   Woman 2: The best place for that is the little cafe on the corner of the market place.
   [Pause . . . Repeat . . . Pause.]

4. Woman: If you want to get to the airport quickly, use the underground, don't take a taxi at this time of day. It takes too long.
   [Pause . . . Repeat . . . Pause.]

5. Woman: Is that lost property?
   Man: Yes, can I help you?
   Woman: I was wondering whether my purse had been found? It's black, with initials in the corner.
   [Pause . . . Repeat . . . Pause.]

6. Man: Can you tell me where the nearest garage is please? I've got a flat tyre.
   Woman: Yes, straight along this road, second left and then you'll see the garage on your right hand side.
   [Pause . . . Repeat . . . Pause.]

7. Man: What shall we do today?
   Woman: Well, there's the museum, the old castle . . . There's a traditional market. Or we could look round the new shopping centre.
   Man: Let's do that – I think we've had enough history this week!
   [Pause . . . Repeat . . . Pause.]

That is the end of Question 9.

You now have half a minute to check your answers. We will tell you when Question 10 begins.

Unit 3 Travel and tourism

Now look at Question 10. *As you can see, this time there are six parts. Imagine that you are in an airport. Listen to the flight announcements and put a tick in the right box – one tick for each of the six parts. You must do this while you are listening because the speaker will not stop and repeat each part separately. At the end, after all six parts are finished, the whole recording will be repeated.*

[Pause] . . . *Now we're ready to start. Listen carefully.*

Woman: Your attention please. Will passengers for flight number YZ 243 to Anchorage please go to Gate number 16; the flight is now boarding. May we remind passengers that first class accommodation is at the front of the aircraft.
    Here is a message for Dominic Andrews travelling with Scandinavian Airtours. Will Dominic Andrews believed to have arrived on a flight from Norway please contact a member of the airport security staff.
    Passengers recently arrived from Amsterdam awaiting the flight to New York in the Transit Lounge should now go to Gate 19 please.
    Flight number XA 268 to Jakarta due to leave at seventeen hundred hours has been delayed. This flight will now leave at seventeen thirty. We apologise for the delay which is due to engine trouble.
    This is a missing child announcement. Will the parents of Mustapha El Ghazi please go to the main desk in the arrivals hall where they will find their son waiting for them.
    Flight BB 159 from Cairo which was expected to arrive at eighteen hundred hours will now arrive approximately one hour late due to poor weather conditions over Northern Europe. Rainstorms have meant delays to all flights and flight BB 621 due to leave for Oslo at twenty-one hundred hours has been cancelled.

[Pause] . . . *Now listen again.*

[Repeat recording.]

You now have a minute to check your answers. We will tell you when the next question begins.

Now look at Question 11. *You will hear a recorded 'Phoneline' information service. You must listen to it and write the correct information in the spaces in your answer book. You don't need to write very much, only a number or a few words. At the end, the recording will be repeated.*

[Pause] . . . *Now we're ready to start. Listen carefully.*

Man: This is the What's On Phoneline for Downhampton and district for

Answer keys

the week beginning Monday the fourth of August.

This week Downhampton Castle is open daily from 9 until sunset. Visitors who would like to join a guided tour of the building should meet the official guide at the West Gate at 11 a.m.

Next, exhibitions. At the City Hall, there is a show called 'Local Artists' of paintings and drawings by students living or studying in Downhampton. At Anderson's Hall in Fitzroy Street you can see a series of fashion photographs by Lisa Wong. That's open every day except Monday from 9.30 until 5.30.

As usual, the Overman collection of antique silver and glass is open to the public on Tuesday and Friday afternoons from 2 till 6.

Special events this week include the Festival of Music from India. Different groups will perform each evening in the great tent in the gardens of Overman House. Performances start at half past seven. Food and drink will be available from half past six, and also after the concert, until midnight.

And that's all from our What's On Phoneline. Thank you for calling.

[Pause] . . . *Now listen again.*

[Repeat recording.]

You now have a minute to check your answers. We will tell you when the next question begins.

Now look at Question 12. *You will hear a taxi driver talking to a passenger. As you can see there are five statements. Listen to the recording and decide if you agree with each statement. If you agree, put a tick in the box under 'Yes'. If you do not agree, put a tick in the box under 'No'. At the end, the recording will be repeated.*

[Pause] . . . *Listen carefully.*
[The conversation is casual but friendly until a misunderstanding sours the atmosphere.]

Man: Where to?

Girl: Ivy Bank Gardens please.

Man: Come again?

Girl: Ivy Bank Gardens –

Man: Oh yeah, I know, you mean near the college?

Girl: That's right.

Man: Okay . . . You a student?

Girl: Yes, I am.

Unit 3 Travel and tourism

Man: What're you studying then?

Girl: I'm going to study Tourism and Hotel Management.

Man: Oh yeah, gonna run a hotel are you?

Girl: I don't think so! But I need to know how hotels are run.

Man: Gonna bring the prices down are you?

Girl: I beg your pardon?

Man: Are you going to make hotels cheaper? Most of us can't afford to stay in them y'know!

Girl: Yes, I know they're expensive. In my country the hotels . . .

Man: Here you are then –

Girl: Is this Ivy Bank Park?

Man: You said Ivy Bank Gardens! By the college.

Girl: No I didn't. I said Ivy Bank Park –

Man: But that's by the university!

Girl: That's right!

Man: Oh gawd! That means I'll have to go all the way round the one-way system. It'd be quicker for you to walk.

Girl: Oh, I'm sorry, but I want to go in a taxi.

Man: Well, look, it's the end of my shift. I was on my way home –

Girl: But I said Ivy Bank Park –

Man: I know but I was doing you a favour really –

Girl: Oh . . .

[Pause] . . . *Now listen again.*

[Repeat recording.]

You now have a minute to check your answers.

That is the end of the test.

UNIT 4 FAMILY, EDUCATION AND SOCIETY

QUESTION 1 One mark for each correct answer

1. Box 1   2. Box 4   3. Box 2   4. Box 3   5. Box 2

QUESTION 2 One mark for each correct answer

1. B   2. A   3. C   4. D   5. B   6. A   7. A   8. D
9. B   10. A

QUESTION 3 Half a mark for each correct answer

1. Y   2. N   3. N   4. Y   5. N   6. N   7. Y   8. Y
9. N   10. N

QUESTION 4 One mark for each correct answer

1. C   2. B   3. E   4. F   5. D   6. A

QUESTION 5 7 marks (1 mark each for 1, 2 and 5; 2 marks each for 3 and 4)

1. Box 3   2. Box 1
3. . . . realise/remember that services cost money.
4. . . . Modern children/They assume education is for everyone/all children.
5. A

QUESTION 6 One mark for each correct answer

1. . . . unable/not able to start . . .
2. . . . does not (usually) have many children.
3. . . . not as big as/smaller than . . .
4. . . . all secondary schools are for boys and girls.
5. . . . are both private and state schools in the system.

QUESTION 7 Total 10 marks

lines 1–9 half a mark for each appropriate and correct completion
line 10 1 mark
line 11 half a mark
lines 12 and 13 up to 2 marks each. See page 63.

QUESTION 8 Total 10 marks See page 64.

QUESTION 9 One mark for each correct answer

1. Box 1   2. Box 3   3. Box 2   4. Box 3   5. Box 2   6. Box 4
7. Box 1

QUESTION 10   One mark for each correct answer

1. Box 3   2. Box 2   3. Box 3   4. Box 3   5. Box 3   6. Box 3

QUESTION 11   One mark each for 1, 3, 5 and 6; 2 marks each for 2 and 4

1. park   2. improved   3. everyone/all   4. sports centre
5. High Street   6. side streets

QUESTION 12   Half a mark for each correct answer

1. Yes   2. No   3. No   4. Yes   5. No

Sample student answer to Question 7

> FIRST NAME   ÇALIK
> SURNAME   AYTEN
> ADDRESS   ELMA SITESI MELTEP SOK
> 80600 ZINCIRLIKUYU-ISTANBUL TURKEY
> DATE OF BIRTH   13.03.1963
> NATIONALITY   TURKISH
> HAVE YOU ANY BROTHERS OR SISTERS?   YES
> WHICH MONTH WOULD YOU LIKE TO VISIT BRITAIN?
> HAVE YOU BEEN TO BRITAIN BEFORE?   YES
> IF YES, WHERE AND FOR HOW LONG?   CHICHESTER
>
> WHAT ARE YOUR HOBBIES/INTERESTS?
> Reading books, walking, listening music, visiting different places, swimming
> DO YOU SMOKE?   NO
> ANY SPECIAL REQUESTS? (eg food, medical care, own room, etc)
> OWN ROOM
>
> WHY DO YOU WANT TO COME TO BRITAIN?   TO STUDY ENGLISH

Suggested mark: $\frac{1}{2}+\frac{1}{2}+\frac{1}{2}+\frac{1}{2}+\frac{1}{2}+\frac{1}{2}+0+\frac{1}{2}+0+1+\frac{1}{2}+1+2=8$

Answer keys

Sample student answer to Question 8

Dear Berrio,

I arrived safely and have already started at language school. It's hard work, but quite interesting for me. I'm pretty busy to study English I'd like to tell you what I am doing a week. On Monday The leson starts at 9·30 in the morning we have Speaking and writting lessons. We have a break for lunch at 12·45. At afternoon our lesson is language through songs.

On Tuesday, we go to library in the morning, in the afternoon our leson is game words.

On Wednesday, in the morning ~~listening and speaking leson~~ We have listening and speaking lessons.

On Thursday, in the morning there are reading and speaking lessons. In the afternoon, we go to museum.

On Friday, we have writing and listening lessons. In afternoon, there are special interest classes.

We must attend morning classes. Afternoon classes and evening classes are open to all those who wish to attend.

I wish you had been here. All my best wishes.
  Yours
    Ayten.

Suggested mark: 4 + 3 = 7

TRANSCRIPT

UNIT 4   FAMILY, EDUCATION AND SOCIETY

Preliminary English Test Listening Test

There are four questions: numbers 9, 10, 11 and 12. Now, look at the instructions for Question 9 only.

As you can see, this question has seven parts, each with four pictures. For each part there will be a short recording, which you will hear twice. You must put a tick in the box under the picture you think is the most suitable.

Unit 4 Family, education and society

Before we start, here is an example:

Boy: What are you doing on Sunday?
Girl: I'm going to church with my parents.

[Pause . . . Repeat as above . . . Pause.]

The girl says she is going to church. So the first picture is the most suitable and the tick has been put in the box under that picture.

Now we are ready to start. Here is a short recording for the first four pictures. Don't forget to put a tick in one of the boxes!

Listen carefully.

1. Woman 1: Is Janet married?
   Woman 2: Yes, her husband's Canadian. And they've got two children.
   [Pause . . . Repeat . . . Pause.]

2. Woman: What's Edward's girlfriend look like?
   Man: She's tall with dark hair – just like his last one!
   [Pause . . . Repeat . . . Pause.]

3. Man: What are you going to do when you leave school?
   Girl: Well, I'd like to work with children so I'm going to train as a nurse in a children's hospital.
   [Pause . . . Repeat . . . Pause.]

4. Woman: Did you enjoy your school days?
   Man: I must admit I did. I was no good at maths or science or anything but I had lots of fun with my friends.
   [Pause . . . Repeat . . . Pause.]

5. Man: Do come and see us one evening. Our flat's very easy to find. You just turn left as you come up the stairs, and we're the second on the right.
   [Pause . . . Repeat . . . Pause.]

6. Man: Did you hear David's won the foreign language prize at school?
   Woman: No! That's wonderful! What was it?
   Man: Well, he had a choice. He didn't need the dictionary or watch, so he took the set of records.
   [Pause . . . Repeat . . . Pause.]

Answer keys

   7. Woman: In next week's class we'll paint something a little more difficult. I'm going to bring in one of my daughter's model cars.

   [Pause . . . Repeat . . . Pause.]

That is the end of Question 9.

You now have half a minute to check your answers. We will tell you when Question 10 begins.

Now look at Question 10. *As you can see, this time there are six parts. Imagine that you're in a language school, listening to the head teacher. He is telling you about the special classes on Wednesday afternoons. Put a tick in the right box – one tick for each of the six parts. You must do this while you are listening because the speaker will not stop and repeat each part separately. At the end, after all six parts are finished, the whole recording will be repeated.*

[Pause] . . . *Now we're ready to start. Listen carefully.*

Man: May I have your attention please? Thank you. Now you've all had a day or two to get used to the school and your classes. I hope everything's OK.

Students: Yes. Thank you.

Man: I'm going to tell you now about the special interest classes that we have on Wednesday afternoons. On Wednesdays, you can choose what you want to do. We put up a list on the noticeboard and you must sign your name under the class you have chosen. Then, at 1.45 on Wednesdays, you go to the room where that class is. Any questions so far?

Student: How do we know which class is in which room?

Man: The teachers will be in their usual classrooms. So Mike will be in Room 7, Nicky will be in Room 4 and Paul will be in Room 2. Except for Philip, who'll be in the language laboratory, and Alison, who'll be in the library. I'll explain why in a minute. OK. So what are the classes? Well there are two sorts, really. Some of them are to give you extra language practice if you want it, and some of them are more general. But all the classes will be good for your English. For example, Philip will be giving you an opportunity to improve your understanding of spoken English. You can go to the language laboratory and he will help you to choose a listening exercise which will suit your particular needs. Alison will be showing slides in the library every week to give you some idea about what you can see if you visit other parts of the United Kingdom. They're very good slides and

Alison will be able to tell you lots of interesting background information. The first week she'll be talking about Edinburgh. Mike will be doing English through song. That's a chance to improve your English and get to know the words of some recently successful pop songs in detail – find out what they really mean! Perhaps even learn to sing them! Nicky is going to do poetry. This will be especially useful for those of you who are taking the literature exam, although anyone is welcome to join, as she will be looking at all sorts of different work. Paul is going to do English for science and mathematics. I know some of you will be going on to study at technical colleges in the autumn, and this could be very useful for you. Lastly, I myself will be doing extra oral practice. We'll do lots of speaking, so it's a chance to improve your accent and practise making some of those awful noises that we here in Britain seem to find so easy! . . . FADE

[Pause] . . . *Now listen again.*

[Repeat recording.]

You now have a minute to check your answers. We will tell you when the next question begins.

Now look at Question 11. *You will hear a recording of part of a meeting to select local government representatives. You must listen to it and write the correct information in the spaces in your answer book. You don't need to write very much, only a number or a few words. At the end, the recording will be repeated.*

[Pause] . . . *Now we're ready to start. Listen carefully.*

Man: Good evening ladies and gentlemen. We'll begin straightaway by listening to the candidates' speeches and I suggest we keep our questions until the end when we've heard all the speakers. Mrs Bradley, would you like to begin –

Answer keys

Woman: Thank you. I don't have much to say and most of you will know my views as I've represented you for the last five years. I'll continue to push for more money for our local hospital as I always have done and my other main interest which is a new play park for our children. We also need to improve the bus service between here and Exeter – not all of us can afford to buy a car – and I shall continue to fight to keep the system of free travel for everyone over the age of 65 – and that's more and more of us in this town. So I hope you'll vote for me when the time comes. Thank you.

Man: Thank you Mrs Bradley. Mr Bennett –

Man 2: Now I know that not all of you will know me as I'm new around here, but that means I've got new ideas. If you elect me as your representative I'll make sure we get a swimming pool and a sports centre. Just what you and your families need! Secondly, this town needs more car parks to avoid the awful traffic jams in the High Street. What's more we need better street lights. The street lamps in the side streets are old and dangerous. If you're going to be out at night you need well-lit streets. Now, I didn't hear Mrs Bradley mention any of these things, so you vote for me and I'll see to it that things will improve.

Man: Thank you Mr Bennett. Now for our third . . . FADE

[Pause] . . . *Now listen again.*

[Repeat recording.]

You now have a minute to check your answers. We will tell you when the next question begins.

Now look at Question 12. *You will hear a girl talking to her parents. As you can see there are five statements. Listen to the recording and decide if you agree with each statement. If you agree, put a tick in the box under 'Yes'. If you do not agree, put a tick in the box under 'No'. At the end, the recording will be repeated.*

[Pause] . . . *Listen carefully.*
[The girl is defensive and truculent, and the mother is anxious and inflexible, while the father seems prepared to discuss the idea reasonably.]

Mum: Have you done your homework yet?

Girl: No, not yet, I want to talk to you and Dad –

Dad: What about?

Girl: About the summer holidays, there's a group of us at school who want to go away together . . .

Mum: Go away together! Whatever next!

Girl: I knew you'd say no.

Dad: Hang on a minute, go away where?

Mum: She's only sixteen!

Girl: That's old enough to get married, so you can't stop me . . .

Dad: Just a minute! Go where?

Girl: France. So we can practise our French.

Mum: Oh yes?! If you want to speak French to each other you can do it here.

Girl: Not to each other. To French people.

Dad: Where'd you stay?

Girl: We'd go camping, there's a camp site in the south of France, Louise stayed there last year with her parents.

Dad: How would you get to the south of France?

Girl: By train.

Mum: Have you any idea how much it'd cost? Who's going to pay for it all? Not that you're going anyway.

Girl: I'll get a job, anyway we haven't worked out yet how much it'll cost.

Dad: Well, I think it'd be a good idea if you get more details and then we'll talk about it again. Okay?

[Pause] . . . *Now listen again.*

[Repeat recording.]

You now have a minute to check your answers.

That is the end of the test.

UNIT 5   PRACTICE TEST PAPER

QUESTION 1   One mark for each correct answer

1. Box 2   2. Box 4   3. Box 4   4. Box 2   5. Box 1

QUESTION 2   One mark for each correct answer

1. A   2. A   3. B   4. D   5. A   6. C   7. A   8. D
9. B   10. A

QUESTION 3   One mark for each correct answer

1. Box 5   2. Box 3   3. Box 4   4. Box 2   5. Box 3

QUESTION 4   Half a mark for each correct answer

1. (0733) 6945   2. (0783) 7860   3. (0358) 72091
4. (0223) 41107   5. 81363   6. (0783) 7892/6042/6207 (any one of these)   7. 32028   8. 35887   9. (0763) 6198   10. (0780) 5453

QUESTION 5   7 marks (1 mark each for 1, 2 and 5; 2 marks each for 3 and 4)

1. Box 1   2. Box 3
3. It/The old car was too small/not big enough.
4. . . . it uses a lot of petrol.
5. A

QUESTION 6

1. . . . influenced by weather conditions.
2. . . . depend on sunny weather in . . .
3. . . . very sunny in southern countries.
4. . . . changeable.
5. . . . very depressed by the weather.

QUESTION 7   Total 10 marks

lines 1–3   1 mark each
lines 4 and 5   up to 3 marks each
line 6   1 mark. See page 71.

QUESTION 8   Total 10 marks   See page 72.

QUESTION 9   One mark for each correct answer

1. Box 4   2. Box 1   3. Box 2   4. Box 1   5. Box 1   6. Box 2
7. Box 2

QUESTION 10   One mark for each correct answer

1. Box 3   2. Box 2   3. Box 4   4. Box 2   5. Box 2   6. Box 4

Unit 5 PET practice test paper

QUESTION 11   Half a mark each for 1, 4, 6 and 7; 1 mark for 2; 2 marks each for 3 and 5

1. 7.07   2. killed/dead   3. burning/on fire   4. south
5. animals   6. 11/eleven   7. 1000/thousand

QUESTION 12   Half a mark for each correct answer

1. Yes   2. No   3. No   4. Yes   5. No

Sample student answer to Question 7

CITY *SPORTS CLUB*

Name Suchie Morinaga

Which sport(s), if any, do you already play? tennis, swimming

Which sport(s) do you want to play with the Club?
  tennis

Are you interested in taking part in competitions? Yes

Please give reasons for your answer Because I would like to know how much improved my tennis ability is, and also It must be exciting if we have any games.

How did you hear about the City Sports Club? I saw an article in the daily newspaper called Chichester

SIGNATURE Suchie Morinaga

Suggested mark: 1+1+1+2+2+1=8

Answer keys

Sample student answer to Question 8

> The Principal
> Wells Language School,
> Somerset.
>
> Dear Ms. Hibbens,
>
> I am writing to enquire about ~~Language schools in Britain~~ your school. I'd like to study English for 3 months in England.
>
> I am studying at the University. My study is finishing in this year. So after finishing my study, I want to go to England.
>
> One of my friends studied in your school last year. She was so pleased that to study in Wells Language School. She suggested that I should go to your school.
>
> Anyway, I'd like to have more information about your facilities Also I want to know how I can ~~have~~ get accommodation. In additional to that, I want to know about your school's fee.
>
> If you inform me about your school, fee, accommodation I'll be very gratefull
>
> I am looking forward to hearing from you as soon as possible.
>
> Yours faithfully,
> Ayten Çalik

Suggested mark: $4+3=7$

TRANSCRIPT

UNIT 5   PET PRACTICE TEST PAPER

Preliminary English Test Listening Test

There are four questions: numbers 9, 10, 11 and 12. Now, look at the instructions for Question 9 only.

Unit 5 PET practice test paper

As you can see, this question has seven parts, each with four pictures. For each part there will be a short recording, which you will hear twice. You must put a tick in the box under the picture you think is the most suitable.

Before we start, here is an example:

Man: Where d'you keep the soap powder?
Woman: In the cupboard under the sink.

[Pause . . . Repeat as above . . . Pause.]

The woman is explaining that the soap powder is in the cupboard under the sink. So the second picture is the most suitable and the tick has been put in the box under that picture.

Now we are ready to start. Here is a short recording for the first four pictures. Don't forget to put a tick in one of the boxes!

Listen carefully.

1. Boy: Which one's your brother?
   Girl: Second from the end in the back row, next to the very tall boy.
   [Pause . . . Repeat . . . Pause.]

2. Woman: Are you interested in buying one of these pictures, sir?
   Man: Well, I rather like that one with the woman at the door with the little cat.
   [Pause . . . Repeat . . . Pause.]

3. Man: Excuse me, are these yours? I think you just dropped them.
   Woman: Thank you very much! I'm always losing things and those are my best gloves.
   [Pause . . . Repeat . . . Pause.]

4. Woman: I have an appointment with Mrs Perkins –
   Man: Oh yes. If you'd like to go straight in, it's down this passage, across the hall, the door next to the lift.
   [Pause . . . Repeat . . . Pause.]

5. Woman: Is that dog yours? He's just run off with my child's ball!
   Man: I'm so sorry, I'll call him back.
   [Pause . . . Repeat . . . Pause.]

6. Man 1: Can you show me how this TV works? I can't get a picture.
   Man 2: Yes, it's the switch at the top – the one in the middle.
   [Pause . . . Repeat . . . Pause.]

Answer keys

   7. Woman: Can you move your car please? I can't open my garage door.
      [Pause . . . Repeat . . . Pause.]

That is the end of Question 9.

You now have half a minute to check your answers. We will tell you when Question 10 begins.

Now look at Question 10. *As you can see, this time there are six parts. Imagine that you are on a tourist trip, listening to a guide describing places of interest. Put a tick in the right box – one tick for each of the six parts. You must do this while you are listening because the speaker will not stop and repeat each part separately. At the end, after all six parts are finished, the whole recording will be repeated.*

[Pause] . . . Now we're ready to start. Listen carefully.

   NOISES OF MOTOR BOAT ON WATER . . .

Man: Good evening ladies and gentlemen, and welcome aboard the boat for this evening's trip along the canal. As we sail along, I'll be pointing out the various sights that can be seen. First of all, on my right you can see the Royal Park – the gardens come right down to the water's edge. The palace is at the far end of the park although you can't actually see it from here. On your left is the oldest wooden house in the town, originally built by a rich merchant and now a museum. Next to that is the famous Little Girl statue erected over 200 years ago. Now, the building on my right belongs to the Jacobsen family and is one of the finest buildings in the whole country, with many valuable treasures and paintings. Opposite on the other side of the canal is the original summer house built by King Odin and now used as a restaurant – very popular with tourists as I'm sure you all know. Next door to that you can see the ruins of a sixteenth century church which was destroyed by fire in the last century – 1843 in fact. Now in the distance, on your right-hand side, you can see the Old Fish Market – looks rather like a castle from here, doesn't it – but this is where the fishermen used to unload their fish each morning for hundreds of years. Today this building is a popular flower market open all the year round. Now if you just look very quickly to your left you'll see . . . FADE

Unit 5 PET practice test paper

[Pause] . . . *Now listen again.*

[Repeat recording.]

You now have a minute to check your answers. We will tell you when the next question begins.

Now look at Question 11. *You will hear a recording of part of a radio news report. You must listen to it and write the correct information in the spaces in your answer book. You don't need to write very much, only a number or a few words. At the end, the recording will be repeated.*

[Pause] . . . *Now we're ready to start. Listen carefully.*

NEWS PIPS . . .

Woman: Good morning, here is the news. Reports are coming in of a serious fire on a train which crashed after leaving Bristol early this morning. The 7.07 Bristol to London train hit another train travelling in the opposite direction shortly after leaving the station. The drivers of both trains were killed. Firemen and ambulance men were immediately called to the scene and police say that a number of passengers have been injured with many more still trapped in the burning trains. The police say it will be at least another two hours before the fire is brought under control.

    The storms along the south coast during the night have brought floods to many small towns and villages. Farmers in the area say that crops have been damaged and many farm animals drowned as the rivers overflowed their banks. Many people are trapped and unable to leave their houses although emergency services are using boats to rescue those people most seriously affected.

    The International Road Race starts from Birmingham at 11 a.m. today. There are over 1,000 people taking part in the competition from all over the world and the centre of Birmingham will be closed to all traffic until eight o'clock this evening. Hundreds of people have already gathered to watch the start of the race and it is expected that before the end of the . . .
FADE

[Pause] . . . *Now listen again.*

[Repeat recording.]

You now have a minute to check your answers. We will tell you when the next question begins.

Answer keys

Now look at Question 12. *You will hear two friends meeting. As you can see there are five statements. Listen to the recording and decide if you agree with each statement. If you agree, put a tick in the box under 'Yes'. If you do not agree, put a tick in the box under 'No'. At the end, the recording will be repeated.*

[Pause] . . . *Listen carefully.*
[The boy is apologetic, then defensive and finally resigned to being in the wrong, whilst the girl is indignant and implacable.]

Boy: Hello, sorry I'm late.

Girl: D'you know what time it is!

Boy: Yes I know, I've said I'm sorry.

Girl: But I've been waiting almost two hours. I rang your parents and they said you left ages ago. Where've you been?

Boy: Nowhere, the bus was late.

Girl: The bus was late! Two hours late! I don't believe you!

Boy: I tell you the bus was late.

Girl: Look, I've been standing here at the bus stop all the time and there've been plenty of buses go past.

Boy: Look I've said I'm sorry, anyway we'd better hurry . . .

Girl: We've missed the beginning of the film. I don't want to go to the film any more anyway. And we were going for a meal before the film . . .

Boy: Well, let's go and have the meal now.

Girl: No thank you. You've spoilt the evening. And what's that you're carrying?

Boy: Cassettes, music cassettes, they're Robert's – he let me borrow them for the weekend.

Girl: So that's why you were late! You went to Robert's house, didn't you?

Boy: Um, um, well I knew you wanted to listen to them so I went to get them as a surprise, it just took much longer than I thought it would.

Girl: Honestly, we could have collected them after the cinema.

Boy: Well, it seemed a good idea at the time – but the way it's turned out has meant no meal, no film and no surprise!

Girl: Well, it's all your fault, if you hadn't . . .

Boy: I know, I know . . .

[Pause] . . . *Now listen again.*
[Repeat recording.]
You now have a minute to check your answers.
That is the end of the test.